RUACH

HA- KODESH

Jen Serrao

Made with ❤ on the Notion Press Platform
www.notionpress.com

RUACH

HA- KODESH

(THE HOLY SPIRIT)

רוּחַ הַקֹּדֶשׁ

"The Spirit of God has made me, and the breath of the Almighty gives me life."

Job 33:4

The Spirit of the Lord is upon me,

Because he has anointed me to proclaim good news to the poor.

He has sent me to proclaim liberty to the captives

And recovering of sight to the blind,

To set at liberty those who are oppressed,

To proclaim the year of the Lord's favor.

Luke 4:18-19

ACKNOWLEDGEMENTS

This book is a gift of the Holy Spirit, By Him, for Him and With Him, to whom belongs all Glory and Honor now and forever.

He also appointed many roles to be part of this journey. It took an immense lot of time and work to get this accomplished and as a strong foundation for much more of this inspiration that is within to be brought forth at the appointed time for it is written that there is a time for every event under heaven.

After God Almighty, who is the creator of all things visible and invisible, the credit goes to my family, for always standing by me as a strong pillar of support. My husband James has been thrilled with this idea of my second book and the first in this genre. He has been utmost supportive, and the best partner God has bestowed me with. I'm proud to be one in spirit with him and always grateful for having such an amazing husband to share my life and godly marriage with.

My children, the anointed prophets, Jaden and Jared, also play my illustrator and editor. The best critics I could have onboard.
Another proud mom moment to have this heritage from God and a godly family.

To Mom Jessy, for all that she has done and all that she does for us.

Talking about family, I cannot miss out on Jasper, our pet Doberman, who gave me good examples to be used in the book and kept his composure when Mama needed to focus on the book.

All my family has in some form, or another been a great source of inspiration and motivation in developing this book. Such a blessing of a blessed and anointed family.

I would like to specially mention all the wise men and women from God from whose guidance and study of the Word, I had better clarity on some of the revelations.

All the below-mentioned people and ministries have made a significant impact on my spiritual journey with the Holy Spirit.

- **JCILM** (Jesus Christ is Lord Ministries), this is where the Word of God was first revealed to me, and the Truth was shared by **Brother Johnson**. This became the foundation for me to continuously aspire, unlearn old teachings, and share my learning with the children of God through various platforms. I also learned and continue learning from this ministry and its works.

- Grace and Graceful Teaching: **Joseph Prince & Priscilla Shirer**
  I would have studied the Word and still lived the legalistic way if Pastor Prince and Priscilla Shirer through the guidance of the Holy Spirit had not shown me the 'Grace' way. Through this Grace revelation, I'm truly saved.

- The Power of the Holy Spirit: **David Hernandez, Kathryn Kuhlman & Pastor Vlad**
  There is nothing more powerful than learning about the power that governs all power. The Power of the Holy Spirit and his identity is amazingly explained through the teachings of these beautiful people from God.

- The Power of the Subconscious Mind: **Rev.Ike, Dr. Joseph Murphy & Dr. Wayne Dyer**
  Unless you realize the exponential capacity of the power within you and the impact it can make, you are just a reader and not a doer of the Word. This is brilliantly taught by Rev.Ike through his visualization prayer techniques and metaphysics simplified by Dr. Joseph & and Dr.Wayne.

- The Power of Prayer- **Dr. Myles Munroe**
  All learning can be futile without knowing the true purpose of our lives. The Kingdom principles and the right way to pray are what I learned the most from this blessed man. His animated series are also one of a kind.

- Biblical Hebrew: **Dr. Bill Barrick**
  The mastery over the Hebrew language and the hidden mysteries are best revealed by this blessed man of God through his Biblical Hebrew series. I loved the Aleph-Bet (Alphabet Song) and Ronni Ronni (Zechariah 2:14) song the most. I always felt that I was part of his classroom though I did the course virtually.

- The Angelic Realm & Power to Prophesy: **Prophet Lovy Elias**
  Power-packed revelations in all his teachings and the prophetic word are just too powerful to resist. A lot of great learnings and applications of truth from his teachings especially on prophesying.

- Power of Words: **Bishop Samuel Patta**
  An intense and powerful teaching of the power of our words that helped me correct my ways of thinking and speaking.

- Gratitude and thankfulness all the time: **Prophet T.B Joshua**
  Understanding that gratitude is important but how can always we be in gratitude is how this prophet unveils some of the kingdom truths.

- It's Supernatural: **Sid Roth**
  From his television series, there is quite a pull to learn and command the power from the Spiritual Realm. In his interactions with different people from God, there is a close encounter with knowing more about these realms.

- Focus on the Family broadcast: **Jim Daly & John Fuller**
  Such immense learning from proficient teachers of Faith across different walks of life to convey one Truth and the importance of a godly family.

This is not a coincidence or a routine that I stumbled upon the teaching of these learned men and women of God. It was all part of the divine plan that was directed for the accomplishment of this book.

Though these saints come from different parts with different ways of teaching, all the revelation comes from only one source, i.e., the Holy Spirit, who also gave me the revelation and allowed me to consult and validate the revelation shared with these saints. To the wisdom that is given to these saints and me, I'm forever indebted to our Glorious and ever-living God.

This is also a means of sharing with the World that though the teaching of the Word comes from the words of these saints, the dependency should always be on the source, the origin of Truth. The glory should always belong to the One True God, who is the Truth.

About the Author

The Holy Spirit, founder, and author of creation is most popular for his work by far on bringing life into existence through the Word. He is not only famous for his role as the **Comforter and Helper** but is the **3rd person of the Holy Trinity.**

The Holy Spirit lives with us and in us (*John 14:17*), as the **Spirit of the Living God** (Christ), whom Jesus gave to us as he was going away until He returned (*John 14:28*)

He is assigned as the **Advocate** to us (*John 14:26*) and teaches us all things and reminds us of everything the Word has said to us.

The Holy Spirit, as our **Comforter (*Romans 8:26-27*)** also helps us in our weakness, interceding for us with groanings too deep for words according to the Will of God.

As the co-author, **Jen Serrao** continues to use her talent of writing after her Debut, " Drop the Not". It's her immense pleasure and honor to work alongside this amazing Author.

She is a wife, a mom to two boys, a corporate professional, and a writer. Apart from her passion for cooking, her forte is in writing. She is a Bible school teacher and facilitates Bible Study on YouTube and other platforms to share the Gospel. Currently, she has been chosen to write this as an inspiration from the Holy Spirit for the glory of His name.

<u>PREFACE</u>

The contents of this book have been developed with careful consideration to the Word of God (all scripture-based) and studied thoroughly, constantly researched, inspired, revealed by the Holy Spirit, and strengthened by the teachings of other men and women of God. For the right understanding, the desire was put in my heart to learn Hebrew, the original language of the scriptures. So, you would see certain references in Hebrew that are meant to bring better clarity and understanding.

This book is not meant to disapprove of religious sentiments of any faith but to confirm the Truth that GOD speaks through His Word, about His relationship with His creation and not religion. It is to unfold the truth in the journey from the Old Testament to the New Testament & and is meant for correcting our older ways of thinking (*2 Timothy 3:16*) and renewal of our minds (*Romans 12:2*).

It is to know and be aware of the existence of the 3 realms (Spiritual, Intellectual & Physical) & most importantly the work of the Holy Spirit, which often is less understood, less spoken of, and less applauded.

It is to know, understand, and apply the power of God working in us for His glory and His purpose. It is about 2 choices that we are presented with but one decision to take.

It is to know the Love, Mercy, and grace of God and to know who He truly is, His desires, His plan, and the Triune (3) God and the 3 parts of our being (Spirit, Soul & Body) and He who makes it come into life (The Holy Spirit).

It is to know who our Faithful God is and to be assured that he always provides what he promises. To understand that His love for us is unconditional (AGAPE). He is our provider, our sustainer, and our ultimate source of provision. He is the Great IAM who chose to be Our Father.

Nothing written in this book can in any form be credited to human wisdom, so I have no credit to take for my works, just being able to glorify God for using my body & and my talents for the purpose He called me to be.

MY CALLING

When I started my journey with the Lord in April 2021, my faith was like Thomas's conditional faith, 'I'll believe when I see'.

Through the process of knowing God and his love for mankind, I realized that Faith which is an unseen substance needs much more than physical sight, it needs spiritual insight.

I had countless testimonies that God provisioned for to strengthen my faith, which then transformed into the faith of Abraham, Noah, and other men of God, who believed in God for who He is and His faithfulness and this led to the renewal of my mind, for now my Faith acts through my works and I see, believe, and receive. While I was making corrections to my old ways, there was another big shift in my lifestyle that I chose to do. Stop listening to the world and listen only to the Word.

This led to a big shift in my thinking process. I realized that the information that I was getting, either from the news or from any informal sources had no reliability.

Plus, I started to self-evaluate further with this question:
- Where am I using this information?

In most cases, the answer used to be,' I'm not using this information anywhere or for any other benefit'.

Information shared and the impact it creates is very important. Information sharing means the use of time and we understand time is money. So, if I waste time listening to or talking about information that I'll not be doing anything about, I'm wasting time and therefore money.

I've also understood that www (the World Wide Web) is truly a snare to distract us from our destiny and purpose. The more we are tagged onto this web, we are trapped. We need to focus on the energy trapped inside us so that we are fulfilling the purpose of God in our lives.

This realization was truly a wake-up call and had a positive impact on my renewal process. 3 years and continuing in the best decision of not watching news/soaps/not engaging in gossip and couldn't feel more energized, more accomplished with the decision I made.

TO THE READER

The origin of this book started with the assumption that I am writing about Him (The Holy Spirit), followed by the correction along the process, i.e. What He wanted me to write about Him.

This book is divided into 3 sections, with great emphasis centered on the number 3 (the number of the Triune God)

The Triune God		The Father
	{	The Son
		The Holy Spirit

3 sections that emerge as:

The 3 Realms		Spiritual
	{	Intellectual
		Physical

Within these 3 Realms, connecting to the 3 parts of our being:

The 3 Parts		Spirit
	{	Soul
		Body

The significance of all 3 (Godhead, Realms, Parts of our being) is intertwined to illustrate co-dependency and working of the unseen into the seen.

In each of these sections, is a revelation to one of the names of the Holy Spirit in Hebrew (RUACH – HA'KODESH)

R – Reading: I now have Knowledge

(HEARER OF THE WORD)

Hosea 4:6 My people are destroyed for lack of knowledge

U – Understanding: KNOW how it can be used (MEDITATE ON THE WORD)

Romans 10:17 So then faith comes by hearing and hearing by the word of God

A – Applying: Using Wisdom to DO the KNOWING (DOER OF THE WORD)

James 1:22 But be doers of the word, and not hearers only, deceiving yourselves

CH – Ches, Chayos – In Hebrew: Life (Bringing the WORD into MANIFESTATION)

Romans 8:11 The Spirit of God, who raised Jesus from the dead, lives in you. And just as God raised Christ Jesus from the dead, he will give life to your mortal bodies by this same Spirit living within you

Through the inspiration of the Holy Spirit **within us**, we will be taught to **READ, UNDERSTAND & APPLY** THE WORD so we obtain the **REVELATION** to **bring forth LIFE**.

Before we step into the teaching, let's start with the illustration of Spirit, Soul & Body

Unseen   **Seen**

Within   *Brings forth*

*1 Thessalonians 5:23 We are a **spirit**, we have a **soul** and we reside in a body*

The **Spirit** commands the **Soul**

The **Soul** listens, receives, and gives instructions to the **Body**

The **Body** obeys

The **Body** through worldly interaction, communicates with the **Soul**

The **Soul** receives from the senses and deposits in the **Spirit**

The **Spirit** filters, retains, and reveals through the **Soul** to the **Body**

All our life we have been chasing or chasing the pleasures of this world, assuming it to give us the peace and happiness that we truly are after.

The revelation provided by the Holy Spirit is for us to have the Truth unveiled from **within us**, for within us is where the Power lies and that **brings forth** the true peace that we desire. He stresses the importance of not searching externally for joy and peace but instead exploring the spirit/the force within you that yields this joy, peace, and many more benefits.

*Luke 17:21: For indeed, the **kingdom of God** is within you.*

When we understand how God created the world, we observe that He created a self-sustaining world, calling (**bringing forth**) into existence things be not as they are (**Romans 4:17**) **from within** from where they existed.

- Seed is **within** the fruit
- Seed **brings forth** the plant and plant **brings forth** the tree
- This means that the Tree is **within** the seed

When we are blessed to be **fruitful, multiply,** and **fill the earth** *(Genesis 1:28)*, we can **bring forth** the fruit from the seed planted **within us.**

The Seed is the Word of God that **brings forth** life.

The Holy Spirit is the giver of life, which means He **brings forth** life, life which is in us for the Spirit of God is **within us**. When God created man and breathed into man His Spirit, His Spirit is **within us** and **brings forth** life.

When I declare, I can do all things through Christ in me (**within me**), I **bring forth** the strength of Christ that enables my weak body to do strong things.

Philippians 4:13 I can do all things through Christ who strengthens me.

When I declare, My God supplies all my needs for He is **within me (Christ – Spirit of God)** and the supply, the abundance (**riches in glory**) **within me** brings forth the supply for every need I have.

Philippians 4:19 And my God will supply all your needs according to His riches in glory in Christ Jesus.

So, the source of everything is in me for God is **within me.**

- New creation/new life (child) comes from within me
- Job comes from within me
- Work comes from within me
- Promotion comes from within me
- Prosperity, wealth, success, good education, good institution, anointed marriage, godly partner all come from within me
- Good Health is in me and the answer to every sickness in this world comes from within me

For mankind came from **within man.**

Every need and every demand can be fulfilled for the power to fulfill is **within me**, for the provision is made for me and in me by the Creator.

Hence, we can do and get what we ask or imagine by His power (immeasurable, beyond our ask and imagination) that is at work **within us**.

Ephesians 3:20-21 Now to him who can do immeasurably more than all we ask or imagine, according to the power that is at work within us, to him be glory in the church and Christ Jesus throughout all generations, forever and ever! Amen.

His power is at work **within us.**

2 Key observations are **Brought forth** and **within us**
For every need/ every desire **within us**, the supply is within us.
The supply can **bring forth** the fulfillment of every need/desire.

*Matthew 6:33 But **seek first the <u>kingdom of God</u> and his righteousness**, and **all these things <u>will be</u> <u>provided</u> for you.***

In Luke 17:21, we learned that the Kingdom of God is **within us**, so if we are seeking the Kingdom of God which is within us, then all these things (food, clothes, and about life) shall be added unto, provided for us or are **brought forth** for us.

Another connection between **bring forth** and **within us** is **The Word**. Wonder why?
When God spoke the Word, it brought forth life, which means that the **Word is a Spirit**. How can, we be sure? Let's understand the word from the Word.

*John 6:63 The **Word of God is Spirit** and it is **Life***

*Hebrews 4:12 For the **word of God** is **alive** and **active***

*Matthew 4:4 Man shall not live on bread alone, but on **every word that comes from the mouth of God***

Now, observe.

W in Word of God and S in Spirit is capitalized – John 6:33 whereas w in Word of God in Hebrews 4:12 is not. Does this imply something?
Whenever any letter is capitalized in a sentence, that refers to reverential capitalization. In this case, both Word and Spirit are nouns. The Word refers to Jesus for the Word became flesh and the Spirit is none other than the Holy Spirit.
This means that the Word of **God** is Spirit (The Holy Spirit) and it is Life (Jesus).

Then, if the word of God is a spirit and we are created in the image and likeness of God, our words are also spirits.
*1 **Timothy 4:14** Do not neglect the **spiritual gift within you**, which was bestowed on you **through prophetic utterance** with the **laying on of hands** by the **presbytery**.*

We are also instructed **not to neglect**:

What: The spiritual gift (within us)
Who: which has been given to us through prophetic utterance
How: with the laying of hands
By Whom By the court composed of Church ministers and representative elders of a particular locality

The Holy Spirit is in 3 forms:

- **Holy Spirit as the Wind**

*Acts 2:2 And suddenly there came from heaven a noise like a violent rushing **wind**, and it filled the whole house where they were sitting.*

- **Holy Spirit as the Fire**

*Acts 2:3-4 And there appeared to them tongues as of **fire** distributing themselves, and they rested on each one of them. And they were all filled with the Holy Spirit and began to speak with other tongues, as the Spirit was giving them utterance.*

- **Holy Spirit as Water**

*John 7:37-39 Jesus stood and cried out, saying, "If anyone is thirsty, let him come to Me and drink. He who believes in Me, as the Scripture said, 'From his innermost being will flow rivers of living **water**.'" But this He spoke of the **Spirit**.*

B)   *INTELLECTUAL REALM (SOUL)*

- Chapter 1: What is the battle for?

- Chapter 2: Understanding our soul

- Chapter 3: Knowing the Destination

- Chapter 4: Understanding our navigation system

- Chapter 5: Open the eyes and ears of the heart

C)   PHYSICAL REALM (BODY)

- Chapter 1: What is the purpose of the Body?

- Chapter 2: Understanding Our Body

- Chapter 3: Understanding the Law

- Chapter 4: Flesh vs Body

- Chapter 5: Union of the Spirit, Soul, and Body

HOLY SPIRIT AS THE WIND

SPIRITUAL

REALM

(SPIRIT)

1

HOLY SPIRIT AS THE WIND

***John* 3:8** *The wind blows wherever it pleases. You hear its sound, but you cannot tell where it comes from or where it is going. So it is with everyone born of the Spirit.*

RUACH in Hebrew (רוּחַ) means **Breath**, **Wind**, or **Spirit**.

In Genesis 2, when God breathed his **Spirit** (the breath of life) into the **dust** he had created, man became a living **soul**. This is also seen in Ezekiel 37, where God is asking Ezekiel to prophesy to the dry bones, first commanding **breath** to enter, then the four **winds.** But without the Spirit, there is still no life in the bones. So once the **Spirit** of God is put inside the people, they will live.

We now understand that the Holy Spirit is the Breath, the wind, and the Spirit that gives life.

Chapter 1: Recognizing who we are
We are the image and likeness of God

א (Aleph)

This is a very important part for the children of God to recognize. One, that there is a **Spiritual Realm,** and second that **We** are a **spirit** for we were created in the **image of God** and **God** is a **Spirit**.

STEP 1: Let's **Read** the scripture to gain knowledge of the Word

Romans 8:9 You, however, are not in the realm of the flesh but are in the **realm of the Spirit**, if indeed the **Spirit of God lives in you**. And if anyone does not have the **Spirit.**

Ecclesiastes 12:7 then the **dust will return to the earth** as it was, and the **spirit will return to God** who gave it.

STEP 2: Understanding of the Scripture (Meditation)

There are 2 conditions attached to the first verse:

- **If** the **Spirit of God lives in us, we** are in **the realm of the Spirit**
- **If anyone does not** have the **Spirit of Christ, they** do **not belong to Christ**

Meditation invites us to ask questions as we are being taught by the Lord (Isaiah 54:17)

- How do we know the Spirit of God lives in us?
- Is there a difference between the Spirit of God and the Spirit of Christ?
- How do we know that the Holy Spirit inspired the Word to be written?

Meditation to me has been a divine experience where you are willing to be taught by the Lord, ask Him these questions and He reveals them to you through His Word. Remember, it's the Holy Spirit who inspired the Word to be written, so always best to check with the Author.

Here's the answer I got to the above question:

- How do we know the Spirit of God lives in us?

Let's see the below verses:

*1 John 4: 12 No one has ever seen God; if we love another, **God lives in us***

*1 Corinthians 6:19 Do you not know that your bodies are temples of the **Holy Spirit, who is in you**, whom you have **received from God**? You are not your own;*

*Galatians 4:6 Because you are his sons, **God** sent the **Spirit of his Son** into **our hearts**, the Spirit who calls out, "Abba,[a] Father.*

From the above verses, we understand that:

- **God is Spirit** (*John 4:24*) and if we obey his commandment of loving one another, the **Spirit of God lives in us**
- If we are **not in the flesh but in the Spirit**, then we have **the indwelling of the Spirit of God**
- **Our Body is a Temple of the Holy Spirit** that **dwells in us** whom we have **received from God**

1. Since **we** are **His children, we** have **the Spirit of His Son**

Wasn't that precious? That's how beautiful and mysterious His Word is. Questions in Answers, Answers in questions.

The Spirit of God very creatively answers the 2nd question too with one of the verses that answered the 1st question.

- Is there a difference between the Spirit of God and the Spirit of Christ?

If we are not in the flesh but in the Spirit = the **Spirit of God** dwells in us

Anyone who does not have the **Spirit of Christ** = they **do not belong to Christ**

Having the **Spirit of Christ** = belonging to **Christ**

Which means having the Spirit of God equals having the Spirit of Christ. So, the conclusion here is that the Spirit of Christ is no different from the Spirit of God.

Also, there is a Spiritual Realm - The realm of the Spirits. Since we now know our identity, i.e being a Spirit, created in the image and likeness of God, who is a Spirit, we are where He dwells, our real home, our Kingdom of Heaven.

Another startling revelation about the Spirit of God is that **Christ** is the name of the **Spirit**. **Jesus** is the name given to the **Body**.

*Matthew 1:21 She will give **birth to a son**, and you are to give him the name Jesus, because he will save his people from their sins.*

And this was to fulfill what the Lord said through the prophet, which is:

*Matthew 1:23 "The virgin will conceive and give birth to a son, and they will call him **Immanuel**" (which means "**God with us**")*

From the above scriptures, we understand that Jesus means **God is with Us in the flesh**. That is why it is said the **Word became flesh**. The **Word was God**.

When we say **Jesus Christ, Jesus** as the **body** and **Christ** as the **Spirit**, we declare ourselves **the Body of Christ**

(1 Corinthians 12:12-27).

When God began his creation:

- He spoke to the **darkness** to bring forth **light**
- Speaking His desire – What He wanted to see (Light) and not what He saw(Darkness)
- He spoke to the **earth** to bring forth **vegetation, seed-bearing plants, and various kinds of trees with seed** in it
- He spoke to the **earth** to bring forth **land animals**
- He spoke to the **waters** to bring forth **sea creatures**
- He spoke to the **sky** to bring forth **birds of the air**
- When He wanted to create **man**, God (Elohim) spoke to **Himself**.
- *"Let **us** make mankind in **our image, in our likeness**"*
- This means if **God is Spirit** and man was created in his image and likeness, then **man is Spirit** too.

It's important to note that Spirits are legal in the Spiritual Realm and if they step out into the Physical Realm, they will need a body.

- So, our **limitless God** placed a **limit on himself** by maintaining **His rulership in heaven** and giving the **rulership of earth to man** (co-heir/partner)
- Now, if **man who is a spirit** needs to operate on earth, he **needs a body to be legal**
- God therefore created the earth suit, which is the **body** made from **earth/dirt/dust** (Adam in Hebrew – means mankind made from dirt) and he brought forth the body from the earth
- God then **breathed his Spirit (Holy Spirit)** into **man** and he became a **living soul**
- So, this **body** of man houses God's **Spirit**, meant for His purpose to be fulfilled on earth, just like it's in heaven

So, when Jesus said that it is good that He is going away so that the Advocate can come to us (*John 16:7*), he meant that **Jesus (Body)** is going away and the **Advocate (Spirit)** will come to us and reside in **our body**, so **we** then become the **body** where **Christ (Spirit) dwells**.

It just amazes me every time how the Word of God begins to be a walk in the maze and through the process always gives us the direction to navigate through the maze.

Moving ahead in getting our 3rd question answered:

- How do we know that the Holy Spirit inspired the Word to be written?

The answer is very well illustrated in the below verses:

- *2 **Timothy** 3:16 All Scripture is **God-breathed** and is useful for teaching, rebuking, correcting and training in righteousness*
- *2 **Peter** 1:20 Above all, you must realize that **no prophecy in Scripture ever came from the prophet's own understanding***
- ***Galatians** 1:11-12 that the gospel I preached is not of human origin. I **did not receive it from any man**, nor was I taught it; rather, I received it by revelation from Jesus Christ.*

From these verses, we understand that the:

- *All* scripture is *God-breathed (**Emphasis mine**)*
- All scripture, not some of it, nor partly but all
- God-breathed which means the breath of God, which is the Spirit of God
- *No prophecy* in Scripture *ever came from the prophet's understanding*
- Again, no prophecy came from the prophet's understanding, and all was from the divine wisdom
- Paul claims that his preaching is *not of human origin*, not received from man nor taught *but received as revelation from Jesus Christ*

This concludes that it's the Holy Spirit and revelation of Jesus Christ that enabled the Word of God to be written by the prophets, not from their understanding or human wisdom.

Now, that we have, 'Read, Understand' the scripture, let's move ahead in our journey.

STEP 3: Applying the scripture

Situation:

Joe was a beggar who sat outside the Church every Sunday, begging for alms. Somedays, he would get a few pennies and some days none. When we went back to his roadside dwelling, he used to surrender all his daily earnings, to his father, who he knew since he was of tender age.

His father was very ill and when he knew his end was drawing near, he called his son and gave him a bowl as inheritance. A few days later, he passed away.

Joe was now alone but was left with the remnant of his father, the bowl. He continued with his begging, this time with the bowl his father had given him.

One day, there was a rich man who passed outside the Church where Joe was begging and spotted the bowl that Joe was using to beg. In anguish, he enquired about Joe and the bowl. He then exclaimed, " Do you even know what you have? Do you even know who you are?"

 Joe with a puzzled look, just shrugged his shoulders and said, "This is my bowl and I'm a beggar".

 The rich man shook him and said, " You are the one and only son of the billionaire in this city. Don't you understand, what you have?" He grabbed the bowl and scratched its surface. While it shone brilliantly, the rich man continued telling Joe, "My owner's son was kidnapped when he was small. This golden bowl was the family's most precious treasure, which was taken along with him. And that son is none other than you."

Our Life Experience:

Don't we relate to Joe? Can we ask ourselves the same questions that were asked to him?

Do we even know what we have and who we are?

Like Joe, we were kidnapped by the power of darkness and made to live in lack, and poverty whereas our inheritance is in the Kingdom of God, with His richness and glory.

The treasure that Joe had, his family inheritance, is the same treasure that has been given to us, the power of the Holy Spirit, who resides in us always. When we don't know who we are, we are

living lives of lack. When we come to the knowledge of the Truth and recognize our Identity, know the treasure we have with us, we live a rich lavish life, just like how the wealthiest heir would live. Because the Truth sets us free. Free from lack, poverty, sickness, and all that belongs to this kingdom, but we are a **Citizen of heaven**, our rightful Kingdom (*Philippians 3:20*)

What we have: The Spirit of God

Who we are: The children of the Most High God, the creator.

We are the IAM of the Great IAM since we are created in His image and likeness. We have the IAM inside of us.

How to Apply it:

1. Take a generous amount of "IAM" affirmations
2. Place them in both your mouth & and heart
3. Confess with your mouth and believe in your heart
4. For best results, repeat this process several times a day and enjoy the blessings

IAM Affirmations

I am the Beloved of God

I am the Child of the Most High God

I am the Body of Christ

I am highly favored, greatly blessed & deeply loved

I am a citizen of Heaven

I am successful

I am prosperous

I am the chosen generation, the royal priesthood

I am fearfully and wonderfully made

I am who He says I am

Chapter 2: Knowing Our Authority

I am the Righteousness of God in Christ

ב (Beth)

- How do we know our Authority?
  - Firstly, we need to know **who we are**
  - Secondly, we need to know **whose we are**.

Both these 'identity' questions seem to have been answered with the previous chapters and we now feel stronger in our knowledge and our identity.

We are the **Body (Jesus) of Christ(The Holy Spirit)** and **belong to God(Elohim).**

So, we are **one** with the **Holy Trinity.**
Elohim: The Hebrew noun אלהים (Elohim, pronounced el-oh-HEEM) is the Biblical Hebrew word for "God." It signifies 3 persons in One God.

Following our rhythm, let's start with the following:

STEP 1: Let's **Read** the scripture to gain knowledge of the Word
*Genesis 1:26 Then God said, "Let Us make **man** in **Our image,**
according to Our likeness**; let them have **dominion** over the **fish of the
sea**, over the **birds of the air**, and **over the cattle**, over [a]all the earth
and **over every creeping thing** that creeps on the earth."*

*Ephesians 1:20–21 **God raised him from the dead** and seated him at
his **right hand in the heavenly places**, far **above all rule and
authority** and **power and dominion**, and above every name that is
named, not only in this age but also in the one to come.*

*Ephesians 2:6 **And God raised us up with Christ** and **seated us** with
him in **the heavenly realms in Christ Jesus**,*

*Luke 10:19 Jesus told us, "Behold, **I give you the authority** to **trample
on serpents and scorpions**, and **over all the power of the enemy**, and
nothing shall by any means hurt you."*

STEP 2: Understanding of the Scripture (Meditation)

Let's read through these verses again and try to find the linkage of
Authority.

Firstly, we were created in the image and likeness of God and given:

- **Authority** (dominion) over all the:
  - *the fish of the sea,*
  - *the **birds of the air**,*
  - *over the cattle,*
  - *all the earth*
  - *over every creeping thing that creeps on the earth*
- Then, we lost **our Authority**, and for it to be restored Jesus had to die (victory over death) and be raised from the dead (access to God and eternal life)
- **Authority of Jesus** when he was raised from the dead
  - *seated at God's **right hand in the heavenly places***
  - *far **above all rule and authority***
  - ***power and dominion**,*
  - *above every name that is named, not only in this age but also in the one to come.*
- **Our Authority and dominion** are restored as we are seated with Him (Jesus) in heavenly places.

  Authority to:

  - *trample on serpents and scorpions,*
  - *over all the power of the enemy,*

STEP 3: Applying the scripture

Situation: Ruby was newly appointed as a police officer. She was a very strong and courageous lady. Her main objective to join the force was to curb crime and make the city a crime-free place. On her 1st day of duty, she wanted to make a good impact and set off on her duty. She noticed some criminals near the dark corners of the road and ran to nab them. As she closed in, they attacked her and left her wounded. She mustered courage to get back to the police station but they didn't seem to recognize her.

She then realized that she was without her badge and was in civilian clothes.

Her bruises made her more aggressive to nab these criminals. She set out for them in the dark corners again. This time when they spotted her, they fled from the spot. She was clad in her police uniform with her badge. She fired her weapon and nabbed them all. She was awarded a bravery award for the courage that she displayed that night.

Our Life Experience:

Relatable?

I could quite relate to her. Most times, we know who we are but choose to face the dark powers, through our works.

They already recognize us as the Children of God but we fail to identify our Identity in Christ and are vulnerable to attack. Without Him, we are just ordinary.

Like Ruby, without the police uniform & and badge, I have no Authority. Without the robe of Righteousness of God in Christ, I'm not backed up. When the dark powers see the Authority in me and the force backing me up, they must flee for I am seated far above all principalities and powers, with the Power of the Spirit working in me, they know I am in charge, in full charge.

How to Apply it:

1. Wear your robe (of Righteousness), presented by Jesus
2. Be sure to pin your badge (the Seal of the Holy Spirit) where it can be seen
3. Be always alert
4. For optimum results, never step out in the dark corners without the robe
5. Enjoy your Authority

So, it's just not about Who we are but whose we are

IAM Affirmations

I am created in the image of God

I am with Authority over all creatures of the earth

I am the one who cannot be harmed by any means

I am the one who has power over my enemy

I am raised with Christ

I am seated in heavenly realms

I am far above all Authority

I am the one who treads on serpents and scorpions

I am the one who can do all things through Christ

I am who He says I am

Chapter 3: Knowing that there is an enemy

God is for you, and it doesn't matter who is against you

ג (Gimel)

Now, that we have progressed with the knowledge of our identity and our authority, it is crucial to know where and when to put it to use. When Jesus gave us Authority *over all the power of the enemy (Luke 10:19)*, he was indicating that **there is an enemy**. In this chapter, we will gain more insights into our awareness of the enemy and who he is.

STEP 1: Let's **Read** the scripture to gain knowledge of the Word

*Ezekiel 28: 14-17 "You were the **anointed cherub** who covers;*

I established you;

You were on the holy mountain of God;

*You **walked back and forth** amid fiery stones.*

*You were **perfect in your ways from the day you were created,***

Till iniquity was found in you.

"By the abundance of your trading

You became filled with violence within,

*And **you sinned**;*

Therefore I cast you as a profane thing

Out of the mountain of God;

And I destroyed you, O covering cherub,

From the midst of the fiery stones. "Your heart was [b]lifted up because of your beauty;

*You **corrupted your wisdom** for the sake of your splendor;*

***Isaiah 14:12-15** "How you are fallen from heaven,*

O [d]Lucifer, son of the morning!

How you are cut down to the ground,

You who weakened the nations!

For you have said in your heart:

'I will ascend into heaven,

I will exalt my throne above the stars of God;

I will also sit on the mount of the congregation

On the farthest sides of the north;

I will ascend above the heights of the clouds,

I will be like the Most High.'

Yet you shall be brought down to Sheol,

To the [e]lowest depths of the Pit.

STEP 2: Understanding of the Scripture (Meditation)

To know about the enemy, we need to know if there is one, if yes, then his source, where he came from, and what was his intent.

So, here's my list of questions for this segment:

1. Is there an enemy?
2. If all that God created was good, who created evil? i.e the enemy
3. What does he want?

Let's begin. Thank you, Holy Spirit, for teaching us.

1. Is there an enemy?

*According to **Luke 10:19**,* Jesus gives us power for the enemy. If there is no enemy, then why give power over the enemy?

So, here's the answer to the question with a question. This is the typical 'Holy Spirit' way (Holy Spirit is very humorous by the way).

Now a bonus to this answer would be:

Exodus 23:22 *If you listen carefully to what he says and do all that I say,* ***I will be an enemy to your enemies*** *and will oppose those who oppose you.*

God said that He'll be an enemy to our enemies, which means it's not just that we have an enemy, we have enemies.

Many such scriptures indicate **there is an enemy,** but these are the key ones. So, the conclusion, therefore, is that **we** not only **have an enemy** but **enemies**.

2. If all that God created was good, who created evil? i.e the enemy

God created the **heavens the earth** and **all creation** and declared it was **good**.

When the heavens were created first, as per Ezekiel 28:14,
- o   **God established** the **anointed cherub**
- o   He was on the **holy mountain of God**
- o   He **walked back and forth** amid fiery stones
- o   He was **perfect** in his ways
- o   From the **day he was created till iniquity was found in him**

- o He became **filled with violence** within and **sinned**
- o He was **cast out** and **destroyed** by God
- o He **corrupted his wisdom** for the sake of his splendor

So, we understand that all that **God created was good,** but the **'anointed cherub' corrupted the wisdom** given by God and **sinned**, thus causing **evil** to take form.

Even in Isaiah 14, we see that it was the cherub's pride to be exalted above God and be like the Most High that led to his downfall from the holy mountain, and he got named Lucifer, which also translates as Morning Star (referred to in Isaiah 14).

We understand that he has been cast out along with **one-third of angels** who rebelled against God. They are referred to as the **fallen angels**.

'Fallen from Grace'

*Revelation 12:4 And his tail drew the **third part of the stars of heaven**, and did **cast them to the earth***

These **stars of heaven** are later referred to as his (Devil) **angels**.

Another scripture to strengthen our knowledge about the fallen angels:

*2 Peter 2:4 God **did not spare** even the **angels when they sinned** but cast them into hell*

- How does evil become the enemy?

Since Lucifer was cast out for his rebellion, he decided to take on God through his children, whom He had created in his own image and likeness. In his rebellion, he has become **an enemy of God and mankind** as Peter states in *1 Peter 5:8* that **our enemy the devil** is prowling like a roaring lion **looking for someone to devour**.

3. What does he want?

Again, per the above verse *(1 Peter 5:8),* our enemy the devil is looking for someone to devour.

Our enemy is looking to devour **our souls**. We will learn as we go, the importance of the soul in the 'Spirit – Soul – Body' study. He is looking to devour our relationship with God and destroy the works of God through us.

As per *2 Thessalonians 2:4,* our enemy will oppose and will exalt himself over everything that is called God or is worshiped, so that he sets himself up in God's temple, proclaiming himself to be God.

STEP 3: **Applying** the scripture

Situation: Jack owned a huge farm. He was wealthy and had huge stocks of cattle and sheep. He had his fields flourishing in all seasons. Suddenly, in one season, his harvest was destroyed. Jack was devastated as he had never experienced such a loss previously. He blamed himself for not taking good care of his crops. He lived in misery and tried to revive his fields but in vain. Every time the crop thrived; the harvest would be destroyed again. He didn't know why this was happening to him. One fine day, his friend came over to meet him after a long time and saw the miserable state of Jack. Having heard and seen his plight, his friend understood the problem. He advised Jack to follow his instructions and Jack followed exactly. In a month, his fields went back flourishing again. Jack's friend helped him understand the rodents who were destroying the crops at night and not active during the day, which is why Jack never knew their existence and kept blaming his work.

Our Life Experience:

All that Jack had to do was know that there was an enemy. Just like Jack, our fields (life, job, health) seem to be destroyed without reason. We (our fields) are attacked, tormented, and condemned but keep feeling guilty and live under constant pressure of not doing enough. When we realize or are being instructed to see the enemy causing this, our paths are now redirected to attack the enemy, revive our fields, and enjoy our flourishing harvest.

When we fail to recognize who we are and/or what our authority is, we are prone to be destroyed as we lack knowledge of our God, who we are in Him, and what he has given us as Authority. While we grow in the knowledge of our identity & and authority, we also need to grow in the knowledge of identifying there is an enemy. Any area where there is no knowledge of these things is highly susceptible to being used by the enemy for his purposes.

Hosea 4:6 My people are destroyed for lack of knowledge

How to Apply it:

1. Sow the right seed in the right soil
2. Water it every day with the Word of God
3. For optimum results, keep guard on the field
4. Be sober, be vigilant knowing that there is an enemy
5. Enjoy your abundant harvest

The Lord teaches knowledge and good judgment.

Chapter 4: Knowing who our enemy is

Overcome evil with good

ד (Dalet)

Once we have realized that we have an enemy, it becomes quite important to know who our enemy is and what are his characteristics.

In this chapter, we will Read and Understand the scriptures alongside.

Read & Understand:
Jeremiah 9:4-6
"Let everyone be on guard against his neighbor,

And do not trust any brother;

Because every brother deals **craftily**,

And every neighbor goes about as a **slanderer**.

"Everyone **deceives** his neighbor

And **does not speak the truth**,
They have taught their tongue to speak **lies**;
They weary themselves of committing **iniquity**.
"Your dwelling is amid deceit; Through deceit, they refuse to know Me," declares the Lord.

From the above scripture, we can outline the different ways that the devil, our enemy is known.

In the **beginning,** the anointed cherub was established as the *'Morning Star'* and **ended** as the *'great dragon, ancient serpent, devil and Satan, the deceiver of the whole world'*.

We understand that the anointed cherub corrupted his wisdom and sinned in his heart, thus transforming into various evil forms.

Let's examine what the scriptures reveal to us:

*1 Peter 5:8 Be sober-minded; be watchful. **Your adversary the devil** prowls around like a roaring lion, seeking someone to devour.*

1.   **Satan, the adversary**: the devil is a legalist
     o   Seeking – Unless we allow him, he has no authority
     o   Adversary - Greek word - Antidikos- one who brings a lawsuit
     o   Anti - Against
     o   dikos- Right

Purpose of Lawsuit: Denying us what is rightfully ours.

Let's further understand this with an example from the Word of God. Where did Satan accuse and whom?

In the Book of Job:

- **Job** was known as **blameless and upright**; they **feared God** and **shunned evil**.
- One day the **angels came to present themselves** before the Lord, and **Satan also came with them**.
- The Lord said to Satan, "Where have you come from?"
- Satan answered the Lord, "From roaming throughout the earth, going **back and forth** on it."

Here's how Lucifer transforms into Satan and why he chose to accuse Job:

Before the fall	After the fall
Lucifer	Satan
Anointed Cherub	Adversary
Blameless	Inequity was found in him, no longer blameless
Going back and forth amid fiery stones	Going back and forth throughout the earth
Going back and forth amid fiery stones, which is in the presence of God, guarding the mercy seat	Going back and forth throughout the earth, bringing a lawsuit, against God's righteous, blameless people like Job

If he was blameless at one point and he now finds God's righteous one, Job is blameless. As an adversary, his case is to prove that Job is not blameless.

2) **Satan as a thief**: The devil is called a thief, so what is he out to steal, kill, and destroy?

*John 10:10 **The thief** comes only to steal and kill and destroy. I came that they may have life and have it abundantly.*

We will understand this better with the help of a parable, Jesus's favorite way of teaching us.

The parable of the Sower that Jesus shared in Matthew 13 about the seeds sown across different soil and their result:

- **Seed sown along the path**: When anyone **hears the message about the kingdom** and **does not understand** it, the **evil one comes and snatches away** what was **sown in his heart**.

- **Seed that fell on rocky places:** One who **hears the word** and **at once receives it with joy**, but since he has **no root**, he **lasts only a short time**. When **trouble or persecution** comes because of the word, he **quickly falls away**.

- **Seed that fell among the thorns**: Is the one who **hears the word**, but the **worries of this life** and the **deceitfulness of wealth choke it**, making it **unfruitful**.

- **Seed that fell on good soil**: Is the man who **hears the word** and **understands it**. He produces a crop, yielding a hundred, sixty, or thirty times what was sown.

The bird always watches for its prey, similarly, the thief always watches for things to steal or the ones to steal from.

Our destiny is to be fruitful (Be fruitful) and our destination (Tree of Life - Jesus), fruit comes from the seed in it and to bear good fruit, our seed must be sown in good soil.

If not, the thief **steals** the seed **kills** our purpose of being fruitful, and **destroys** our relationship with God.

(Seed) Word of God = Sowed on the path/among the weeds/rocky grounds **(hears and not doers)** = Not fruitful

(Seed) Word of God = Sowed in good soil **(the heart)** = Good harvest and Fruitful

3)   Satan's role of serpent:

*Revelation 20:2 He seized the dragon, that **ancient serpent, who is the devil, or Satan**, and bound him for a thousand years*

Again, a startling revelation in Genesis with the **serpent** and again being spoken about in Revelation in the above scripture.

We are now taught that:

- The first sin was committed by Lucifer, the anointed cherub thus becoming Satan, the devil.
- Sin corrupted his anointed nature and was cast out from heaven, being referred to as the Father of the fallen angels
- His only motive was and is:
    - to corrupt the anointed nature of God's image and likeness created in mankind
    - to get mankind to sin and destroy the image that they were created into ensure mankind does not fulfill the right purpose they were created for

Now, let's unfold the **truth** about the **lies** of the devil.

- God created the whole creation and called it **good**
- **Provided** for all of mankind's **needs** before creating **mankind**, whom he called **very good**
- **Provision before** the **need**
- Put **mankind in charge** to take care of the garden
- **Permission** to **eat from all trees** and **prohibition** to **not eat from only one tree** of the knowledge of good and evil
- In the middle of the garden were the **Tree of Life** and the **Tree of the Knowledge of Good and evil**
- This implies they were **destined to eat from the tree of life** and **live an eternal life**
- **The Tree of Life** was in the **middle** of the garden and denotes the **center person** the **Holy Trinity**, i.e **Jesus**, who is also known as the **Tree of Life**

In the words of God to Adam, *"You are free to eat from **any tree in the garden;** but you must **not eat from the tree of the knowledge of good and evil,** for when you **eat from it** you will **certainly die."***

- How did sin enter the garden?

Sin needs a body to manifest since we learned that spirits need a body to operate legally on Earth. Since Adam and Eve were already in the knowledge of God, who is good, they hadn't known any evil.

So, sin had to choose a body to communicate with them.

Here's how and why sin enters through the serpent.

We read in Genesis 3:1 that the **serpent** was **more crafty** than any of the wild animals the Lord God had made.

Crafty means the "ability to do anything, Sin used this craftiness of the serpent as **skillful** at **deceiving** others.

Related verse: Luke 20:23, Jesus perceives "the craftiness" of His adversaries.

The serpent therefore became a fine choice for sin to enter as Satan could now corrupt the wisdom of mankind through the serpent and fulfil his motive.

- How does Satan lie?

*"Did God **say**, 'You must not eat from any tree in the garden'?"*

*"You **will not certainly die**," the serpent said to the woman. "For God knows that when you eat from it your **eyes will be opened**, and you will be like God, knowing **good and evil**."*

- Satan lies by:
  - Challenging God's command - *Did God **say***
  - Stating half-truth - *You must **not eat***
    Truth: The command was to eat from all trees except one
  - Opposing God's Word - *You **will not certainly die***
    Truth: The consequence was *You will certainly die*
  - Stating the fact *that eyes will be opened Truth:*
  - *Genesis 3:7, Then the eyes of both of them were opened*
  - Deception: *you will **be like God Truth:*** Adam and Eve were already created in the image and likeness of God and were like God
  - Deception: *knowing **good and evil***
    Truth: They had only one, God who was good and there was only destiny – Tree of Life. By disobeying they would allow sin to enter and have the knowledge of both good (God and all that he created) and evil (Satan and his fallen angels)

So, Satan's motive was fulfilled as he deceived Eve, with Adam following Eve's request to eat the forbidden fruit and get expelled from the garden just as he was expelled from the holy mountain.

We also understand that wisdom and knowledge of Eve are corrupted when she contaminates God's command by adding the below:

*"You must not eat fruit from the tree that is in the middle of the garden, and **you must not touch it**, or you will die."*

God had not mentioned about not touching the tree. So, this is how deception plays.

In the below scripture, we are alerted by St. Paul on deception and the man of lawlessness (Satan) being revealed.

*2 **Thessalonians** 2:3 Don't let anyone **deceive** you in any way, for that day will not come until the rebellion occurs and the man of lawlessness is revealed, the man doomed to destruction.*

    4)   **Satan as a murderer**
***John 8:44** You are of your father the devil, and your will is to do your father's desires. He was a **murderer** from the beginning and does not stand in the truth, because there is **no truth in him**. When he lies, he speaks out of his own character, for he is a liar and the **father of lies**.*

Satan is a **murderer** from the beginning, and this is how he entices the children of God.

In Genesis 4, when God accepts Abel's sacrifice and not Cain's, he cautions Cain by saying:

*So, the Lord said to Cain, "Why are you **angry**? And why has your **countenance fallen**? 7 If you do well, will you not be accepted? And if you do not do well, **sin lies at the door. And its desire is [d]for you**, but you should rule over it."*

Despite the instruction/caution given by God, Cain in his free will allowed sin to enter the door and devour him. Instead of ruling it, he was ruled by it and like Satan who was the murderer, through this enticing, lured Cain into becoming a murderer too.

*Genesis 4:8 Now Cain [a]talked with Abel his [b]brother; and it **came to pass**, when they were in the field, that Cain rose up against Abel his brother and killed him.*

One more follow-up question with the words, 'came to pass'.

- How can Abel's murder be something that has come to pass?
- Was it plotted? Was it prophesied?

We know that God was warning Cain about sin desiring him but why did God not warn him about what sin was planning to do?

Sin always means evil and evil means sin. Sin is an act of Satan to make us disobey God, thereby disconnecting us from our

relationship with God. Satan's motives are already known to God, who is omniscient.

Satan committed the first sin, and he was now roaming, walking back and forth for someone to devour, he was lurking outside Cain's door, desiring to rule over him.

God knew Lucifer's desires then as he sinned in his heart, and he knows Satan's desires now.

God who knew that Satan was a murderer from the beginning, therefore, instructed Cain to not let sin rule over him and in turn make him a murderer.

God also knew that the murder would be committed (it came to pass) just like he knew that Lucifer would become Satan by sinning.

We need to know that our God is a God who has given us freedom and the will to make choices. The same free will he gave Lucifer, the same that he gave mankind, and the same that he gives us.

So, though God knows what we are exactly going to do, he desires to always protect us from the evil one.

He directs our paths and lets us choose. He showed Cain not to take the wrong path, however, it was Cain's choice/free will to give Satan/sin to seek him and devour him.

We can also see God's mercy spilled across this chapter, which is not easy to see in the chaos of this situation.

- If God didn't care, he wouldn't have bothered to alert Cain of sin's attempt to rule him.
- God is aware of Satan's motives and was offering advice to Cain as he wasn't aware of Satan's schemes.

*2 Corinthians 2:11 so that Satan might not **outwit** us. For we are not unaware of his schemes*

- God was disciplining and teaching Cain on the acceptable sacrifice, so he could overcome anger on not being accepted and learn to make the 'sweet aroma' sacrifice.
- God protects Cain by placing divine protection on him, thus preventing anyone from killing him.

What I love the most about this scripture is that God was talking to Cain, which means though sin blocked the presence of God, he always chose and chose to be with his children.

5) Satan is a father of lies: *Satan has **no truth** in him, he is a **liar**.*

In the same Cain incident, Cain not only committed the first murder but also lied.

Then the LORD said to Cain, "Where is Abel your brother?" He said, "I do not know. Am I my brother's keeper?"

He lied about not knowing his brother's whereabouts.

So, God was not only alerting Cain that sin was not only desiring him through **anger** and **murder** but also about **lying** and not **repenting**.

Satan must have used lies to lure his angels to follow him in his rebellion against God and used the same lies with Cain.

He must have told Cain,

- Did God favor Abel's sacrifice and not yours?
- Didn't God tell you that you are the seed that will crush the serpent's head?
- Your sacrifice will never be accepted until Abel is alive.
- He is standing in your way by stealing your position to rule.

This may have caused his anger and his countenance to fall and further lies in that order must have made Cain commit the grievous sin.

6)   **Satan as the slanderer:** Slander would mean telling the truth, but that truth would be meant to hurt.

*Leviticus 19:16 You shall not go about as a **slanderer** among your people, and you are not to act against the life of your neighbor; I am the Lord.*

In the Garden of Eden, he slandered God's character.

He told the truth about God prohibiting them from eating the fruit but corrupted it by adding that God didn't want mankind to be like Him.

There are many scriptures in the Bible about not slandering. So, our command is to stay away from slander.

7)   **Satan as the tempter**

*Matthew 4:1 Then Jesus was led by the Spirit into the wilderness to be **tempted** by the devil.*

As a thief, Satan comes to steal. No thief comes to plunder an empty house. So, if you are attacked/tempted/tormented, you should realize that you are the powerhouse of treasure and the thief is out to plunder the treasures.

That's the same context of the above verse when Jesus was tempted. In his 30 years on earth, he was not tempted or attacked, however the moment he was baptized and had the treasure of the Holy Spirit in Him, he shone like a powerhouse of treasure, attracting the thief to this prosperous house.

The temptation immediately follows the anointing.

Matthew 4:1-11Then Jesus was led by the Spirit into the wilderness to be tempted[a] by the devil.

Another beautiful revelation in this verse is:
*Jesus was **led by the Spirit** to be **tempted by the devil**.*

- Jesus was led not taken or followed which means Satan needs to be permitted or allowed to tempt
- Those led by the Spirit of God are the children of God

*Romans 8:14-17 For those who are **led by the Spirit of God** are the children of God.*

- When did the devil tempt?
  - When Jesus in the flesh was most vulnerable after fasting for forty days and forty nights and was **hungry**.

- All the 3 temptations were **of the World but from the Word**

- o "If you are the Son of God, tell these stones to become bread." - *Deuteronomy 8:3*

- o "If you are the Son of God," he said, "throw yourself down." For it is written:
'He will command his angels concerning you,
and they will lift you in their hands, so that you will not strike your foot against a stone.' – *Psalm 91:11-12*

- o "All this I will give you," he said, "if you will bow down and worship me." - *Deuteronomy 8:19*
- One more thing to be noted is in the previous verse where Jesus is baptized, God calls him, **'my Beloved Son'**, and just verses later, Satan addresses Jesus as the **Son of God**, omitting the most important word, **Beloved**.
- Satan was once the anointed angel, who is well versed with the scriptures as he quotes them when tempting Jesus.

Here's a summary of knowing the enemy – Satan in his different evil forms.

1. **Satan, the adversary**
2. **Satan as a thief**
3. **Satan's role as serpent**
4. **Satan as a murderer**
5. **Satan as a father of lies**
6. **Satan as the slanderer**
7. **Satan as a tempter**

STEP 3: Applying the scripture

Situation:

Joshua is 85 years old and insists on taking his wife hand in hand wherever they go.
When he was asked by a passerby as to why his wife was so distracted.
He replied: She has Alzheimer's.
When asked, "Will your wife worry if you let her go?"
He replied, " She doesn't remember. She doesn't know who I am anymore, she hasn't recognized me for years."
When asked again, " you continue to guide her on the way every day even though she doesn't recognize you? " The elderly man smiled and said, " She doesn't know who I am, but I know who she is ".

" SHE IS THE LOVE OF MY LIFE "!"

Our Life Experience:

If this is the unconditional love of this man towards his wife, just imagine how much more our Heavenly Father loves us.

Just like this old man, who for years without any expectation has been faithful to his wife, holding her hand lest she go astray, our Father holds our hand knowing that we have forgotten who He is or what He has done for us and are vulnerable to go astray.

Most times, we want to go a different route than where He is taking us, we want Him to let go of our hand so that we can be 'free' to go our way. But this freedom that we are being lured to is a snare set for us by the devil.

Satan in different forms is out there to get us but with God holding our hand and willing to be led, we are protected. If God is for you and with us, who can be against us? Even if they are against us, can the enemy prevail? Never in eternity. For our God has promised us that no weapon formed against us shall prosper.

How to apply?

FAITH CHALLENGE FOR LIFE:

Guard Your Mouth and Speak words aligned to the WORD OF GOD

- I choose to multiply (*) my blessings
- I choose to subtract (-) my worries
- I choose to divide (/) myself from the worldly desires
- I choose to add (+) more saved souls into the Kingdom of God

MEDITATE ON THIS SCRIPTURE:

Exodus 4:12 Now go; I will help you speak and will teach you what to say.

Chapter 5: Understanding the enemy's strategies

Fight of Good Faith

ה (Hei)

We have come quite far in our journey from knowing who we are, to knowing there is an enemy and who the enemy is. With the revelation of the Truth so far, we are continuing our journey into the Battle Ground, now understanding what the enemy's strategies are.

STEP 1: Let's **Read** the scripture to gain knowledge of the Word

*Matthew 16:23 Jesus turned and said to Peter, "**Get behind me, Satan!** You are a stumbling block to me; you do not have in mind the concerns of God, but merely human concerns."*

*Acts 5:3 Then Peter said, "Ananias, how is it that **Satan has so filled your heart** that you have **lied to the Holy Spirit** and have kept for yourself some of the money you received for the land?*

John 4:1 Beloved, do not believe every spirit but **test the spirits** to see whether they are **from God**, for many false prophets have gone out into the world.

Luke 22:3-4 Then **Satan entered Judas**, called Iscariot, one of the Twelve. And Judas went to the chief priests and the officers of the temple guard and discussed with them **how he might betray Jesus**.

Luke 22:31 And the Lord said, Simon, Simon, behold, **Satan hath desired to have you**, that he may sift you as wheat

STEP 2: Understanding of the Scripture (Meditation)

As a warrior on the battlefield, it's not sufficient if I just know:

- who my enemy is
- what his character is

If I don't know the strategies of the enemy, I am as good as an untrained warrior.

Let's meditate on the essence of these scriptures, one by one:

1. *Matthew 16:23 Jesus turned and said to Peter, "**Get behind me, Satan**! You are a stumbling block to me; you do not have in mind the concerns of God, but merely human concerns."*

- Why did Jesus say this to Peter?
- What did Jesus see that made Jesus address Peter as Satan?

Let's look at the context in which Jesus said this:

In Matthew 16:17-19, Peter declares that Jesus is the Messiah, again not revealed by flesh and blood, but by our Father in heaven. Jesus also declares that he will give him the keys to the kingdom of heaven.

So, what changed between verse 19 to verse 23, was that Peter who was commended for his declaration of Jesus was suddenly referred to as Satan.

From verse 21 onwards, Jesus predicts his death and explains to his disciples about their plight and that He must die and be raised to life on the third day.

To this, Peter rebukes Jesus by saying "Never, Lord! This shall never happen to you!"

With sin entering Earth through Adam's disobedience, the only way to redeem and restore mankind to its original design was through an obedient sinless man, who could take the sins of all the world on Him and serve the judgment/wrath that mankind is worthy of.

Like, we learned earlier, body was required for legal activity on earth and so God (Spirit) chose to come in through His Son in the body of Jesus. Now, this makes a lot more sense, when we read Emmanuel (God with us).

Now, when this is the planned mission of God to rescue mankind, Satan who was aware of this had to block it somehow. So, he chose Peter to be used to stop Jesus from continuing his mission. Because, if he accomplished making Jesus not go to the cross and die, we would still be dead in sin and Satan would triumph in his victory. Little does he know, that God who created him (Satan) is well aware of his evil schemes, and through Jesus rebukes Satan in the body of Peter to get behind Him.

Like Jesus, how can we identify that, it's not the person but Satan using them for his evil plot?

- Anything or anyone that contradicts the Word of God is from Satan or is Satan

The Word of God says in:

Genesis 3:15 *"And I will put enmity*

Between you and the woman,

And between your seed and her Seed;

He shall bruise your head,

And you shall bruise His heel.".

But, what did Satan say through Peter - Never, Lord! This (death and resurrection) shall never happen to you.

This is how Jesus was able to see through the acts of Satan using Peter.

An important observation is God mentioning enmity between Satan's seed and her (woman's) seed.

Based on the nature of the body function, there is no seed from the woman. So, when the reference is being made to her seed, its God's seed came as Jesus through the body of Mary, because remember we were taught a body is needed for legal activity on Earth. It's also the prophecy of virgin birth.

The first prophesy of warfare between good and evil, is where God declares victory in the beginning.

He (Jesus) will bruise /crush your head (Satan), and you will bruise his heel (nailed to the cross).

That is victory over death/sin which didn't originate in mankind before being corrupted by Satan, through deceiving Eve. So, God through his prophesy was restoring everything to, "**Good**" as in the beginning, with the **death** (death of sins of the whole world and consequences of sins – death, sickness, lack, etc) and **resurrection** (right standing with God, justification through the Finished works of Jesus), His Beloved Son.

We are taught through his ways, how we can rejoice in our victory (our redemption) planned before creation.

*Matthew 1:20 Joseph, son of David, do not fear to take Mary as your wife, for that which is **conceived in her is from the Holy Spirit***

With this scripture, we understand that which comes from the Holy Spirit brings forth life.
Remember, our most famous act of the Holy Spirit in the creation in *Genesis 1,* where the Holy Spirit was hovering over the waters, it brought forth Life.

We further understand in *John 6:63 that it is the Spirit who gives life*.

2. ***Acts* 5:3** *Then Peter said, "Ananias, how is it that **Satan has so filled your heart** that you have **lied to the Holy Spirit** and have kept for yourself some of the money you received for the land?*

Just like how Jesus identified Satan in Peter, in this verse, Peter identifies Satan in Ananias.

If we are willing to be taught, then we can catch the methods that Jesus used, to understand the patterns of Satan.

If we fail to choose and are not willing to be taught, then Satan will make the choice, fill our hearts and make us lie to the Holy Spirit – The Spirit within us, for he is the Father of lies and that is all he can teach.

3. ***John* 4:1** *Beloved, do not believe every spirit but **test the spirits** to see whether they are **from God**, for many false prophets have gone out into the world.*

While we are finding patterns in the works of satan to unearth his strategies, God is instructing us to test the spirits and see if they are from God or not.

Let's check the Word of God to find out the truth to substantiate this:

*1 John 4:2-6 By this you know the **Spirit of God**: every spirit that confesses that Jesus Christ has come in the flesh is from God, and every spirit that does not confess Jesus is not from God.*

Every spirit that confesses that Jesus Christ has come in the flesh	**PASS** THEY ARE FROM GOD
Every spirit that does not confess Jesus	**FAIL** THEY ARE NOT FROM GOD

By this instruction, here's how you can conduct this test:

4. *Luke 22:3-4 Then **Satan entered Judas**, called Iscariot, one of the Twelve. Judas went to the chief priests and the officers of the temple guard and discussed with them **how he might betray Jesus**.*

Everybody on earth is designed for a purpose defined by God.

The first and foremost thing we ought to do is understand the purpose of our existence.

Judas's body was used by Satan to drive his purpose. Betrayal of Jesus would mean his successful crucifixion and death of Jesus, which would be an end to the motives of Jesus to bring about redemption.

Did Judas allow Satan to take charge of him?

Let's understand from the scripture again:

John 12:6 He said this, not because he (Judas) cared about the poor, but because he was a thief, and having charge of the moneybag he used to help himself to what was put into it.

So, we understand that Judas was not a righteous man, he was a thief, which made him an accomplice to the acts of Satan, who was seeking to devour him at the right time.

The same Jesus who identified Satan in Peter and addressed him as Satan, now calls Judas a friend, whom Satan enters, when he betrayed Jesus and got Him arrested. Both had Satan acting on them.

Matthew 26:50 Jesus replied, "Do what you came for, friend.

What's going on?

If we read it with a clear mind, we understand that any stumbling blocks in the mission of Jesus, he would regard that as Satan blocking his work. When Peter rebuked him and became a stumbling block in his mission, he referred to him as Satan.

However, though he knew Satan had entered Judas, and was trying to get him closer to his mission that had to be fulfilled, he called him friend, because he was not a stumbling block but helping him fulfill his mission. God planned this mission and orchestrated the

the whole event from the plan for redemption and restoration of mankind, creation, destruction of mankind, birth, death, and resurrection, fulfilling all prophesies.

One observation I had was how come a plan for redemption precedes creation, shouldn't it be after the destruction/after sin entered? By now, we know the first sin was committed by Lucifer on the holy mountain. We also know our God is a God outside the beginning, for he created the beginning. He plans beginning from the end. His ways are not our ways and his thoughts are not our thoughts.

5.   *Luke 22:31 And the Lord said, Simon, Simon, behold, **Satan hath desired to have you**, that he may sift you as wheat*

Doesn't this pattern look familiar?

" **Satan** hath **desired to have you**" and the verse from Genesis 4:7 **sin** lies at the door. And its **desire** is for **you** or desired to have you.

Jesus is trying to point out the patterns in Satan so we are well aware of his evil schemes and just as He overcame temptation, we are well capable of fighting this battle with the Word of God.

Chapter 6: Spiritual Warfare

Wearing the Whole Armor of God

ו (Vav)

By now we are aware of our position, both on the battlefield and in God. We are aware of our enemy and his possible patterns and strategies. Now, it's time to get set for our weapons of spiritual warfare.

In this chapter, the Holy Spirit will guide us to use these weapons and fight the unseen enemy.

Sounds quite captivating right?

To start with, let's ask a question:

- How do we know a tree is good or bad?
    - By its fruit, right?
- How does the tree stand firm?
    - By its roots right?

In this visualization, we can see the tree/the fruit but cannot see the roots. However, the roots control the growth/destruction of the tree.

Bottom-line, what is **seen** is **controlled by the unseen**.

Therefore, it becomes highly imperative for us to understand the Spiritual Realm, the power of the unseen and how can we learn the right controls.

STEP 1: Let's **Read** the scripture to gain knowledge of the Word

*2 Timothy 2:25-26 Opponents must be **gently instructed**, in **the hope that God will grant them repentance** leading them to a **knowledge of the truth**, and that they will **come to their senses** and **escape from the trap of the devil**, who has taken **them captive to do his will.***

Let's break this scripture down:

- We, the opposition to the enemy **must be** gently instructed
  - Must be – not an option
- Instructed in the **hope** that God will grant us **repentance**
  - Hope of repentance

  One of the observations in Genesis after the fall of Adam and Eve is that they never repent. They didn't walk to God instead walked away and hid from God.
- This leads us to the knowledge of the truth
  - Knowledge of Satan's lies
- We will come to our senses
  - Which means we weren't in our senses
- Escape from the trap of the devil
  - Through the strategy that God will teach us, we will learn to escape from the snares of the evil one

- The Devil has taken us captive of his will
  - When we had earlier lost the battle, we were taken captive to do his will and with the redemption that we've received through Jesus, we are now free and no longer captive

There is something beautiful that is starting to unveil with the Holy Spirit teaching us and revealing the knowledge of truth. Be ready **for eyes to be opened**.

*2 Kings 6:17 Then Elisha prayed and said, "O Lord, please **open his eyes** that he may see." So the Lord opened the eyes of the young man, and he saw, and behold, the mountain was full of horses and chariots of fire all around Elisha.*

*Luke 24:31 And their **eyes were opened**, and they recognized him. And he vanished from their sight.*

*Genesis 3:7 Then the **eyes of both of them** were opened, and they knew that they were naked, and they sewed fig leaves together and made themselves coverings.*

What's the revelation here, you may wonder?

The opening of eyes doesn't relate to the natural senses, i.e. the physical realm but the Spiritual senses in the Spiritual Realm.

Let's see it from both perspectives, physical and spiritual:

Physical Realm	Spiritual Realm
2 Kings 6:15 When Elisha's servant **saw (physical sight)** the horses, chariots, and a great army, that had surrounded the city sent by the King of Syria, he asked his master what to do.	*2 Kings 6:16* Elisha responded by stating, " Do not fear, for those who are with us are more than those who are with them." When Elisha prayed for his (servant's) **spiritual eyes to be opened**, he (servant) saw the mountain was full of horses and chariots of fire all around Elisha.
Genesis 3:7 Then the eyes of both were opened, and they knew that they were naked. After the fall, **the physical eyes** of Adam and Eve were opened, which is why they saw the reality of the physical world (their nakedness)	*Genesis 2:25, Now the man and his wife were both naked, but they felt no shame* In the Spiritual Realm, there is no gender, only in the physical realms, male and female are the names given to the body. Man is the name of the spirit

Luke 24:16 But their eyes were restrained, so that they did not know Him. After the resurrection of Jesus, 2 of the apostles were walking together, conversing about Jesus's resurrection but their eyes were restrained, so that they did not know Him.	*Luke 24:31 Then their eyes were opened and they recognized him, and he disappeared from their sight* Their eyes were restrained earlier, however at the appointed time, their hearts burned as they realized that the Messiah was with them through their Spiritual eyes

Now, aren't our spiritual eyes opened to see the reality of the Kingdom of God and what great treasures he has stored up for us? Most importantly, the treasure of His Word. Thank You Holy Spirit for revealing the Truth of your Word, so that we are well able to see only the Truth (our strongest weapon) and not the lies of Satan (his fiery darts).

There is a special purpose of numbers in the Bible. We were provided this revelation of the **Number 3**, which represents the Triune God.

Number 7 is another beautiful revelation of completeness.

God completed his work on **the seventh day (7)** and called it **Finished** just as Jesus Christ completed his mission and after shedding his precious Blood in **7 places** and with **His 7 words**, called it **Finished**.

Psalms 76:3 There he broke the flaming arrows of the bow, the shield, and the sword, and the weapons of war. Selah.

So, how do we use this number of completion in warfare?

And here's the revelation by our Holy Spirit:

*Ephesians 6:14-18 Stand firm then, with the **belt of truth** buckled around your waist, with the **breastplate of righteousness** in place, 15 and with your **feet fitted with the readiness that comes from the gospel of peace**. 16 In addition to all this, take up the **shield of faith**, with which you can extinguish all the flaming arrows of the evil one. 17 Take the **helmet of salvation** and the **sword of the Spirit**, which is the word of God. And **pray in the Spirit** on all occasions with **all kinds of prayers and requests**.*

The first readiness during warfare is to have strong armor. We are now about to see (with our spiritual eyes) this important weapon of Spiritual Warfare.

Let's learn about wearing the Whole Armor of God.

Where was this first used?

Isaiah 59:15-18

Truth is lacking, and he who departs from evil makes himself prey.

The LORD saw it, and it displeased him

that there was no justice.

He saw that there was no man,

and wondered that there was no one to intercede;

then his arm brought him salvation,

and his righteousness upheld him.

He put on **righteousness as a breastplate**,

and a **helmet of salvation** on his head;

he put on **garments of vengeance** for clothing,

and wrapped himself in **zeal as a cloak**.

According to their deeds, so will he repay,

wrath to his adversaries, repayment to his enemies;

to the coastlands, he will render repayment.

The Armor God Gives Is The Armor God Wears

"Through the gospel, the divine warrior gives us his equipment, which he wore first in our place."

- When do we use armor?
- What if don't use the armor?
- How should we use it?

1 Thessalonians 5:8 But let us, who are of the day, be sober, putting on the breastplate of faith and love; and for a helmet, the hope of salvation.

What are the 7 pieces of armor of God?

1. The Belt of Truth.
2. The Breastplate of Righteousness.
3. The Gospel of Peace.
4. The Shield of Faith.
5. The Helmet of Salvation.
6. The Sword of the Spirit.
7. Prayer in the Spirit

1. Belt of Truth

When do we use a Belt? To secure or hold up clothing together, right? Devil, the Father of Lies, uses his strongest weapon of lies against us. If we aren't secured with the Belt of Truth, his lies can strip us from other weapons, for Truth is the only strongest weapon that can undermine the lack of knowledge that he uses to destroy us.

2. Breastplate of Righteousness

The breastplate serves as a protection for some of the most important parts of the body.

Underneath the breastplate is the heart that needs to be protected against the wiles of the enemy.

When we were once sinners, the devil used his weapons of condemnation and instilled self-doubt in us. Now, that we are made the righteousness of God in Christ, the breastplate of being in right standing with God should protect us, especially our hearts.

3. Fitted Feet

Feet are meant to take us places to preach the Gospel of the Lord. Fitted feet are feet rooted in the Word of God, meant to keep us on the right path and lead others on this path too.

If our feet waver from the paths of righteousness and truth, we become an easy target for the enemy and so he attacks our feet. But are feet are meant to tread on serpents and scorpions and continue the journey of Truth using this weapon.

4. Shield of Faith

A shield is another defensive armor to protect the front of the body when attacked. Then devil plans to keep us away from Truth, condemns us and attacks our Faith. If we stay rooted in Faith and don't yield to his motives but let the shield protect us, we are covered.

5. Helmet of Salvation

The helmet protects your head from external attacks. Beneath the head is the mind that is constantly attacked/tormented through thoughts the devil tries to invoke to make us prone to his attacks. If we wear the helmet of salvation which is to be confident that we are saved and therefore not allowing anything else to penetrate through the helmet to the mind.

6. Sword of the Spirit

The sword can be used for cutting or striking the enemy in warfare. It is often used as a symbol of honor and authority.

While all other armor that we have is **defensive - guarding ourselves against the tactics or schemes of the devil**, the Sword of the Spirit is both a defensive **and offensive warfare weapon - tearing down the strongholds that the enemy has formed in your mind through deception and accusations**. When Jesus was tempted, He used the Sword of God's Word, i.e. the Spirit to strike back. We need to adopt the same battle tactic of pulling down evil strongholds by using the Sword of the Spirit and also for taking thoughts captive and setting minds free.

7. **Prayer**

Prayer enables children of God to fight mighty battles in the unseen realm. Like the Sword of the Spirit, this is also a defensive and offensive weapon. And if you top this weapon with another mighty weapon, which is Praise and Worship, the enemy doesn't stand any chance.

When Israel faced a mighty enemy, they began to sing praises to God, and He set an ambush to defeat their army. This is the same method we need to adopt.

Let's also understand what part of the armor God doesn't want us to wear when we fight.

If we see his armor that he handed down to us, the only part missing is the **garment of vengeance** for, *"vengeance is mine"* says the Lord (*Deuteronomy* **32:35**)

So, we understand and honor our Father's request for being able to fight the good fight of path wearing the full armor of God but not wearing the garments of vengeance.

Warfare is ready, Armor is ready. Before we wear the whole armor of God, He gives us certain instructions:

- Finally, **be strong in the Lord** and **his mighty power**.
- **Put on the full armor of God**, so that you can take your stand against the devil's schemes.
- For our struggle is **not against flesh and blood**, but **against** the **rulers**, **against** the **authorities**, **against** the **powers of this dark world**, and the **spiritual forces of evil in the heavenly realms**.
- Therefore **put on the full armor of God**, so that **when the day of evil comes**, you may be **able to stand your ground**, and **after you have done everything, to stand**
- Finally, **be strong in the Lord** and **his mighty power**.

What does it mean to be strong in the Lord and his mighty power?

- **Put on the full armor of God**, so that you can take your stand against the devil's schemes.
  Why full armor when we stand protected by God?

- For our struggle is **not against flesh and blood**, but **against** the **rulers**, **against** the **authorities**, **against** the **powers of this dark world**, and the **spiritual forces of evil in the heavenly realms**.

Our struggle is not against flesh and blood:

When Jesus celebrated Peter for recognizing Him as the Messiah, he also stated that it wasn't revealed to Peter by **flesh and blood** but by our Father in heaven.

In the same chapter, Matthew 16:21, Jesus called Peter Satan as he recognized that it was not **flesh and blood** (Peter)but Satan whom the struggle was up against.

- **Spiritual forces of evil in the heavenly realms**.
- Therefore **put on the full armor of God**, so that **when the day of evil comes**, you may be **able to stand your ground**, and **after you have done everything, to stand**

Emphasis on putting the full armor of God

Why?

so that **when the day of evil comes**, you may be **able to stand your ground, after you have done everything, to stand**

2 Corinthians 10:3-5 For though we live in the world, we do not wage war as the world does. The weapons we fight with are not the weapons of the world. On the contrary, they have the divine power to demolish strongholds. We demolish arguments and every pretension that sets itself up against the knowledge of God, and we take captive every thought to make it obedient to Christ.

We are in this world but not of this world, which means in the Spiritual Realm, the weapons we fight with and wage war against are not like the world does.

We have divine power to:

- demolish strongholds,
- demolish arguments
- demolish every pretension that sets itself up against the knowledge of God

When we fight with these spiritual weapons, we take captive every thought to make it obedient to Christ.

So, war is won, and victory is achieved when:

- We follow the instructions of God on how we ought to fight the battle with spiritual weapons
- We wear the full armor of God
- We demolish strongholds and every act of the dark forces and take every thought captive in obedience to Christ

Chapter 7: Our strategy to win the Battle every time

Be strong and courageous

ז (Zayin)

Winning and being victorious is our inheritance as the children of God.

However, the enemy can be very convincing and appear as though they are on your side, making it difficult to distinguish flesh and blood vs forces of darkness in the spiritual realm. As it is written in the scriptures even Satan transforms himself from the' devil of darkness' to an 'angel of light'.

2 Corinthians 11:14 Even Satan disguises himself as an angel of light.

Therefore, it becomes commanding for us to constantly be victorious by being prepared, being vigilant, and standing firm and strong in the Lord.

Let's take examples from the Word of God which teaches us how we can win every time in the Spiritual Warfare

Isaiah 54:17 No weapon that is formed against thee shall prosper; and every tongue that shall rise against thee in judgment thou shalt condemn.

2 Chronicles 32:7-8 "Be strong and courageous, do not fear or be dismayed because of the king of Assyria nor because of all the horde that is with him; for the one with us is greater than the one with him. With him is only an arm of flesh, but with us is the Lord our God to help us and to fight our battles."

Proverbs 21:31 The horse is prepared for the day of battle, But victory belongs to the Lord.

Firstly, know that **there is a weapon that is being formed against you**. This is exactly the purpose of the enemy.

Secondly, know that we are backed up by a strong force that declares that **though the weapon is formed it cannot prosper.**

When you know no weapon formed against us will prosper and victory belongs to the Lord for the one with us is greater than the one with the enemy. And the Lord our God helps us to fight our battles we can rejoice in the Lord always.

It's an example of any battle. From the scriptures, if we take the battle that David fought against Goliath and the Philistines, his weapons were 5 pebbles.

David declared victory before he began the battle, He knew the force backing him up.

It was not what was in his hand (5 pebbles) that mattered but God's power in Him, the grace (5 is the number of favor/grace)

that made him victorious. So, it's **not how much we have** that makes us victorious **but who we have in us** that declares us victorious.

Let's look at David's faith and his confidence.

Goliath's armor	David's armor
<ul><li>Bronze helmet on his head</li><li>wore a coat of scale armor of bronze weighing five thousand shekels</li><li>On his legs he wore bronze greaves</li></ul>	Shepherd's tunic with a staff in his hand and a shepherd's bag

Goliath's weapons	David's weapons
• Bronze javelin was slung on his back • Spear shaft was like a weaver's rod, and its iron point weighed six hundred shekels • Shield bearer went ahead of him.	A sling and a stone; without a sword in his hand

Warrior Experience – Goliath	Warrior Experience – David
A warrior from his youth, challenging the army of Saul to fight against him	Shepherd boy keeping his father's sheep. When a lion or a bear came and carried off a sheep from the flock, he struck it and rescued the sheep from its mouth. When it turned on David, he seized it by its hair, struck it, and killed both the lion and the bear

Confidence of Goliath	Confidence of David
<ul><li>Choose a man and have him come down to me.</li><li>If he can fight and kill me, we will become your subjects;</li><li>but if I overcome him and kill him, you will become our subjects and serve us."</li><li>This day I defy the armies of Israel! Give me a man and let us fight each other</li><li>Goliath cursed David by his gods, "Come here," he said, "and I'll give your flesh to the birds and the wild animals</li></ul>	<ul><li>Who is this uncircumcised Philistine that he should defy the armies of the living God</li><li>Let no one lose heart on account of this Philistine; your servant will go and fight him</li><li>The Lord who rescued me from the paw of the lion and the paw of the bear will rescue me from the hand of this Philistine</li><li>You come against me with sword and spear and javelin, but I come against you in the name of the Lord Almighty, the God of the armies of Israel, whom you have defied.</li><li>This day the Lord will deliver you into my hands, and I'll strike you down and cut off your head.</li><li>This very day I will give the carcasses of the Philistine army to the birds and the wild animals, and the whole world will know that there is a God in Israel. - All those gathered here will know that it is not by sword or spear that the Lord saves; for the battle is the Lord's, and he will give all of you into our hands</li></ul>

Thus, David won the victory not on his own accord but by Faith in the Lord, for the battles belong to the Lord and so does victory.

There is also a secret formula I want to point out.

James 4:7 *Submit to God and Resist the devil and He will flee from you*

Let's put it as a formula now:

1+1=2

Everyone is familiar with this equation:

Here, this equation would mean:

1(First process step) + 2 (Second process step) = Result

Submit to God and resist the devil = He will flee from you.

Now, most times, we hate going through the process, and just want results and that is far from impossible. We also try to alter the result however it should be altering the process.

It's as simple as following all the steps to a recipe to get an amazing dish.

It could also mean:

1(God's part) + 2 (Our Part) = Result

Always the constant + Variable (Our faith that can waver) = Determines the result

In this situation of David, which approach did he follow:

1 (Lord delivered Goliath into David's hands) + 1 (David struck him down and cut off his head) = David's victory over the Philistines and saving Israel

In all these secret formulas, one part is always static and 100% accurate, that is God's part, for He is always faithful to His Word.

So, in this situation, if David hadn't followed the equation fully, he wouldn't get the result.

For example, God had already done his part:

- Lord delivered Goliath into David's hands

Now, if David had declared that it was by his works and not in the name of the Lord Almighty, he is not completing his part and the result couldn't have come to pass or if we spoke in fear and not in faith, the result wouldn't have been achieved, the battle wouldn't have been won.

In the Spiritual Realm, the Lord had already delivered Goliath into David's hands, for the Word to manifest in the Physical Realm, David had to activate the Word by Faith.

Through his declaration of God's Word, he called things that are not as they are (*Romans 4:17*) and brought victory into manifestation in the Physical Realm.

A good learning for us is to understand that no matter how big/powerful (Goliath) our situation may be, we rejoice in the victory for we know the result of the situation (Goliath's disastrous end).

Let's also look at other such successful formulas that marvelously worked with these key warriors:

- Abraham
- Noah
- Isaac
- Joseph
- Moses

2 things common among them were **Faith** and **Prayer**. Both are unseen substances.

FAITH: *Hebrews 11:1 - Now faith is the assurance of things hoped for, the conviction of things **not seen**.*

The Hebrew word for faith is אמונה (Emunah) and is an action-oriented word meaning "support". This is important because ideally, the concept of faith places the action on the you have faith in, such as "faith in God". But, the Hebrew word אמונה places the action on the one who "supports God". It is not a knowing that God will act, but rather I will do what I can to support God.

This reminds me of a powerful message by one famous evangelist:

- Without God, man cannot
- Without man, God will not

This again takes us into remembrance of the secret sauce, the equation:

$$1+1=2$$

God's action + man's support = Faith in action

PRAYER: *Philippians 4:6–7 Do not be anxious about **anything**, but in **everything** by **prayer** and **supplication** with **thanksgiving** let your requests be made known to God. And the peace of God, which surpasses all understanding, will **guard your hearts and your minds** in Christ Jesus.*

The Hebrew word tefillah (תפלה) comes from the verb parallel (פלל), "to judge".

Tefillah comes from the Hebrew word l'hitpalel, which stands for the process of accounting or contemplation, as well as "to judge oneself". In Exodus 21:22, l'hitpilim is used to refer to **executing judgment.**

Prayer is, therefore, a **petition** to the heavenly judge who executes judgment and involves contemplation or self-evaluation.

The prayer template that Jesus gave us, 'Our Father' is composed of **seven petitions**.

There are **three** "thy-petitions" (thy name, thy kingdom, thy will) followed by **four** "us-petitions" (give us, forgive us, lead us not, and deliver us).

Through these key virtues of Prayer and faith, let's see how they transformed the lives of these Godly men.

Men of God	Faith according to the Word of God
Noah	*Hebrews 11:7 By **faith** Noah, being divinely warned of things **not yet seen**, moved with godly fear, prepared an ark for the saving of his household, by which he condemned the world and became heir of the righteousness which is **according to faith***
Abraham	*Hebrews 11:17 By faith Abraham, when God tested him, offered Isaac as a sacrifice. He who had embraced the promises was about to sacrifice his one and only son, 18 even though God had said to him, "It is through Isaac that your offspring will be reckoned."* *19 Abraham reasoned that God could even raise the dead, and so in a manner of speaking he did receive Isaac back from death*
Isaac	*Hebrews 11:20 By faith Isaac blessed Jacob and Esau concerning the future.*
Moses	*Exodus 17:12 But Moses' hands grew weary; so they took a stone and put it under him, and he sat upon it, and Aaron and Hur held up his hands, one on one side, and the other on the other side; so his hands were steady (emunah)until the going down of the sun.*
Joseph	*Hebrews 11:22 By faith Joseph, when his end was near, spoke about the exodus of the Israelites and gave instructions about his bones*

These were a few instances of a few chosen men who demonstrated their Faith in action.

Important to note is the **place and time of their promises** coming to pass according to their Faith. What is the learning for us from this and how can we apply it?

Men of God	Evidence of Faith	Promise Fulfilled
Noah	Did everything that God commanded him without seeing any trace of the floods that God foretold	Noah & and his household were saved from the floods and another promise that God would never curse earth nor destroy any living creature
Abraham	Obeyed and circumcised every male of his household as per the covenant set between God and him	Isaac was born to Abraham and Sarah in their old age. Everything happened **at the time** God had said it would
	Left his country, his relatives, and his father's family for the land God showed him	Promised Land as his inheritance and blessed in every way
	In obedience, offered his one and only son at the altar	Blessed with offspring multiplied as the stars of heaven and as the sand that is on the seashore, possessing the gate of their enemies

Isaac	Though too blind and weak to distinguish between his two sons, by the power of the Holy Spirit, he blessed Esau and Jacob and spoke words about the future of their families	Blessed generations, Isaac, with his father and son, will be seated in the kingdom of God
Moses	Chose to be ill-treated by the people of God rather than to have the temporary enjoyment of sin	Chosen and given the ability to set the Israelites free
	Picked up & and used the staff as instructed	Empowered to fight and win battles and lead the Israelites into salvation
	Led the people across the Red Sea	Passed through the Red Sea as though they were passing through dry land; and the Egyptians, when they attempted it, were drowned
Joseph	By not succumbing to temptation posed by Potiphar's wife and not sinning against God	Ultimately became ruler of the land, second only to King Pharaoh

People of God	Petition (Prayer)	Promise Fulfilled
Abraham's servant	"O LORD, God of my master Abraham," he prayed, "please grant me success today, and show kindness to my master Abraham"	Before the servant had finished praying, Rebekah came out with her jar on her shoulder and was declared to be the bride of Isaac
Isaac	He prayed to the LORD on behalf of his wife because she was barren	The LORD heard his prayer, and his wife Rebekah conceived twins
Hannah	"O Lord of hosts, if You will indeed look on the affliction of Your maidservant and remember me, and not forget Your maidservant, but will give Your maidservant a son, then I will give him to the Lord all the days of his life, and a razor shall never come on his head."	The Lord answered her petition and gave her a son

In the Spiritual Realm, we are Spirits, and our **words** are **Spirits**. So, every word we speak brings forth life or death as indicated in *Proverbs 18:21*.

Death and life are in the power of the tongue; and they that love it shall eat the fruit thereof.

From the tongue comes words and words have power. So, this is a great weapon to always use and be victorious with the enemy in the Spiritual Warfare, provided we use the words taught by the Word of God.

Like Spirits, words are not seen. To win the battle every time, we must make sure we are born again with the Spirit.

Born again?

Isn't this the same inquisitiveness that Nicodemus had when he asked Jesus how can one be born again?

John 3:3 Jesus answered him, "Truly, truly, I say to you, unless one is born again he cannot see the kingdom of God."

Let's dive into that question – How can we be born again?

1 Peter 1:23 *For you have been born again, not of perishable seed, but of imperishable, through the living and enduring word of God.*

- We have been born again
- not of perishable seed, i.e Adam who inherited the consequence of disobedience, both spiritual and physical death
- The imperishable seed is through the living and enduring word of God, i.e through Jesus Christ and his accomplished work for mankind

Since it's our spirit that has been born again and not the soul or the body, it becomes quite important for the Spirit to be trained (**to act according to the Word**) to not get strayed as the Body and Soul can (**by the World**).

With what we have Read and Understood, we need to learn how to apply **Training the Spirit**:

Before the training, let's start with **Warm Up**:

- God is a Spirit
- We are a Spirit
- Since God is Spirit, we need to worship Him in spirit and truth (***John 4:24***)

Begin Training:

- Keep the instruction/Word of God always on your lips

- Meditate on the Word of God, Day and night (Pray in the Spirit)
- Be careful to do everything written in it **Result: Prosperous**

How do we know our spirit is renewed or we are born again?

Here's the, **'born again'** test:

- Are you still impacted by defeating situations?
- Do you still allow people to impact your thinking of who they think you are?
- Do you still live a life of lack?

If the answer to the above is "No" for all questions, then congratulations,
'You are born again in Spirit'

If otherwise, you need to unlearn and renew your Spirit man with the Truth we learned in the previous chapters.

As we learn about the Spiritual Realm, it's very important to learn about the Angelic ministry. For these are divine beings given to man to help with our purpose.

Hebrews 1:14 calls angels "ministering spirits" sent to serve those who will inherit salvation.

In *Psalm 91:11* We are advised of angels concerning us, who are commanded to guard us in all our ways; lift us in their hands, so that we will not strike our foot against a stone.

The **devil** will try to block our purpose by distracting us, attacking us, tormenting us, and causing stumbling blocks in our path.

It's these **angels** given to us who minister to us, guard us, and remove every block that prevents us from getting to our destination.

Our Lord is the Lord of heavenly hosts (angels) and as it is written in *Matthew 18:10* angels in heaven always see the face of my Father in heaven.

So, when we understand the presence of these angels, we glorify the presence of God, who has appointed them for us.

IAM DECLARATIONS WHEN FACED WITH ADVERSITY:

- IAM THE ONE WHO COMES AGAINST YOU(**ADVERSITY**) IN THE NAME OF THE LORD ALMIGHTY
- IAM THE ONE IN WHOSE HANDS THE LORD WILL DELIVER THE ENEMIES (**PROBLEMS**)
- I AM THE ONE WHO WILL HAVE YOUR HEAD (**EVIL ACTS**) CUT OFF WITH MY SWORD (SWORD OF THE SPIRIT)
- I AM THE ONE THROUGH WHOM THE WORLD WILL KNOW **THERE IS A MIGHTY GOD**

HOLY SPIRIT AS FIRE

INTELLECTUAL

REALM

(SOUL)

2

HOLY SPIRIT AS FIRE
Esh (אֵשׁ)

is the Hebrew word for fire. Fire is generally used as a metaphor to indicate God's wrath, torment in hell, destruction, etc. However, with the right understanding and discernment, we can observe that when the Holy Spirit came upon the apostles, tongues of fire rested upon them. The same apostles who were scattered upon Jesus's death and lived in fear were filled with boldness once they were baptized by fire.

Holy Spirit as fire does the same thing in our lives. Gives us the boldness to speak, lights up our lives with the Truth expelling darkness/lies, and convicts us to refine our souls and in the process brings up all the old thinking and impurities on the surface, ready to be filtered out.

Chapter 1: What is the battle for?
The battle is not yours but God's

ח (Chet)

Psalm 55:18 He will redeem my soul in peace from the battle which is against me

From the previous teaching, we are now sure:

- There is an enemy
- Who the enemy is
- Who we are and our authority
- Of the enemy's strategies
- Of the war waging, weapons being formed
- Of our strategies to fight and be victorious

But, God who is so good and made everything good, why is He preparing us for this battle with His armor, what is this battle all about? Let us understand why the battle.

From the verse Psalm 55:18, we understand that God is all for redeeming our soul from the battle that is against us, from the weapon that is formed against us, so that neither the weapon formed nor the battle planned will prosper against us but only our souls shall prosper.

It's now clear that the **battle is for our souls**.

What's special about it is that both God and Satan are fighting for it and there is a battle for it.

Feel special, don't you? A war specifically for our soul!

Let us dwell more in His Word to find out more about our souls.

Ecclesiastes 12:7 Then shall the dust return to the earth as it was: and the spirit shall return unto God who gave it

- Dust is nothing but our dirt **body**, the earth suit which shall **return to** where it came from **Earth**
- **Spirit returns to God**, who breathed it into the body

*Genesis 2:7 Then the LORD God **formed a man from the dust of the ground** and **breathed into his nostrils the breath of life,** and **the man became a living soul.***

Dust of the ground (Body)

Breath of life (Spirit)

Man became a living (Soul)

So, then what happens to the living soul?

In 1 Peter 2:11 it is written *"Beloved, I urge you as aliens and strangers to abstain from fleshly lusts, which wage war against the soul."*

This means there is a war that is being waged against the soul and there is a consequence for the souls that lose. If we note the verse below, it'll give us more insight into **who owns the souls**.

*Ezekiel 18:4 Behold, **all souls are Mine;** the **soul of the father** as well as the **soul of the son is Mine. The soul who sins will die.***

So, we understand that it's the **Lord God declaring that all souls are His** and **the souls of those who sin will die**.

When God created us, He created us with free will, a free choice on how we employ our souls.

God's motive is only to save our soul and protect it from the evil one. He gives us the necessary guidance so we can choose to follow his will and do his purpose to save our souls. The soul is the one encountering judgment and so it's important to safeguard our souls with the Word of God.

Chapter 2: Understanding Our Soul

Our Soul belongs to the Lord

ט (Teth)

Now that we know that the battle is against our soul, much important to understand why.

- What would anyone gain from obtaining our soul?
- Why only the souls of humans and not of other creation?

For these questions to be answered, we will have to break down the soul components.

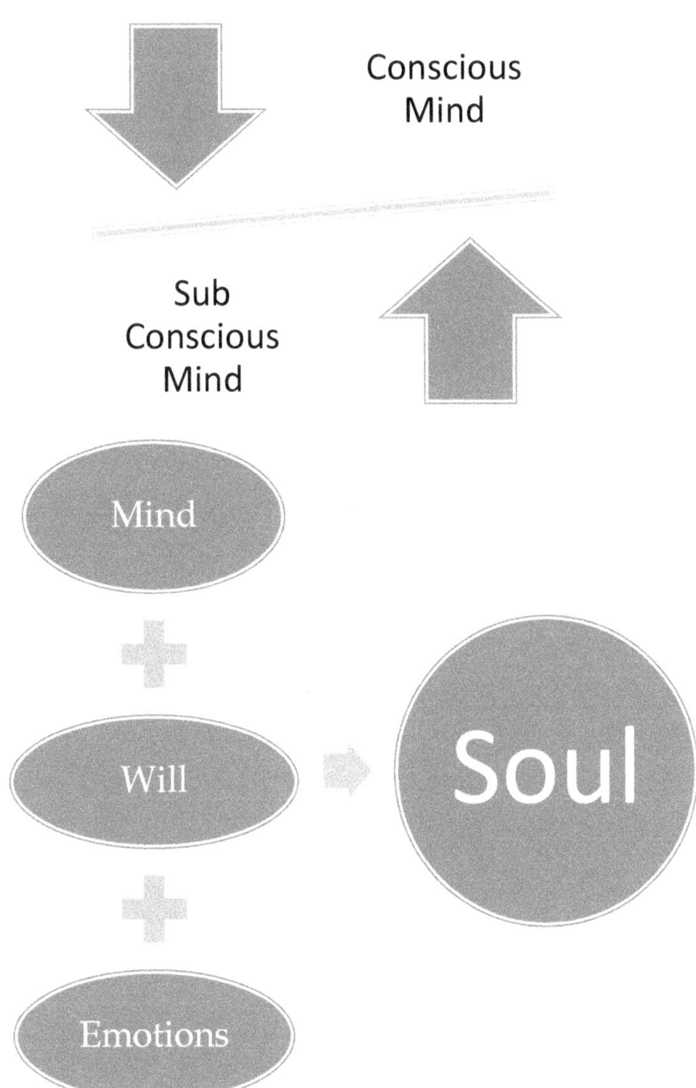

Conscious
Mind
Sub
Conscious
Mind
Mind
Will
Emotions
Soul

Now, let's see the process of creation:

- God created heavens and earth
- God brought forth day and night
- God brought forth the sky, land, and seas
- God brought forth vegetation from the land, seed-bearing plants, and various kinds of trees that bear fruit with their seed
- God brought forth seasons, sun, moon, and stars
- God brought forth living creatures, birds of the sky, animals of the land, and creatures of the sea
- Then, God created mankind in his image and brought forth mankind from within Him

So, what's different in the creation of man vs other living creatures and creation?

Distinctive qualities of mankind:

- **God** created **man** in **His image and likeness**
- **God brought forth man** from **Himself**
- **God breathed** into his nostrils the **breath of life** and **man** became a **living soul**
- **God** gave **man dominion** over all the fish of the sea, birds in the sky, and every living creature that moves on the ground
- **God** commanded **man** to **subdue** the earth
- Subdue means "to place in order"

So, God was looking for someone to manage Earth. Just like things were, "not in order" before He created (*Genesis 1:2 Now the earth was formless and empty, darkness*), He wants us to get 'things in order" for we are created in His image and likeness to imitate Him.

The most distinctive feature of man vs the rest of the creation is that man has the breath of God, which sets Him apart and so Satan is not after other creation but the one that was created in God's image, i.e man

So, this distinctive feature of man called, the 'Soul' comprises of Mind, Will, and Emotions.

- o What is **Mind?**

One of the Greek words for mind is phroneo is used frequently, most often translated as mind (meaning thoughts, reasoning, or views)

In *Matthew* 22:37, when Jesus quoted, "*Love the Lord your God with all your **heart** and with all your **soul** and with all your **mind**.*", he fairly distinguished these 3 (heart, soul, and mind).

So, in conclusion, the Mind is the storehouse of our thoughts, reasoning, and viewpoints.

Like in the Spiritual Realm, we learned that eyes were opened (Spiritual eyes), in the below verse, we also understand that minds also need to be opened to perceive the truth.

*Luke 24:45 Then he **opened their minds to understand the Scriptures***

In the previous verse, Jesus appears to the Apostles after his death and tries to explain that it's 'Him' but their minds are still in doubt.

He then had to **open their minds** so they could understand the scriptures and the fulfillment of the law that He was conveying to them.

What does the **Mind** comprise?

- Conscious Mind
- Sub- Conscious Mind

Conscious Mind focuses attention on all that we actively experience through our senses, i.e. See, Hear, Taste, Smell, Feel (All 5 senses).

It captures thoughts based on what we see, hear, imagine, taste, smell, and feel.

- When I **see** beautiful scenery, I exclaim, " Wow, such amazing scenery"
- When I **hear** a pleasant sound, I would be delighted and say, " That's an awesome rhythm"
- When I **taste** something exquisite, I close my eyes and allow the taste sense to speak, "Mmmm, this is the most flavorful dish I've ever had"
- When I **smell** a good fragrance, my overpowered senses with closed eyes would say, "Just mesmerizing"
- When I **feel** the cool breeze on a hot afternoon, my senses would again speak, " Just the caress I needed"

With all these senses and their feelings, it's the thoughts speaking. However, these thoughts may or may not be retained in our memory. However, there is the subconscious mind which stores every detail that has been passed through by the conscious mind.

Sub-Conscious Mind It took until recently for me to figure out that **heart** means **Subconscious Mind**. My Spiritual eyes and mind were also opened, so I could understand this underlying Truth.

This is the most strategic part of the soul and how we control it determines the course of our journey.

In the chapters to follow, we will get to the heart of the matter.

*Proverbs 4:23 Above all else, **guard your heart**,*

*for **everything** you do **flows from it**.*

Let's read it again:

- o Above everything else
- o Guard your heart (subconscious mind)
- o For everything you do
- o Flows from it

So, the words of wisdom are for us to guard what enters our subconscious mind, for all that gets deposited there is what flows from us. This is emphasized by another scripture.

Luke 6:45 A good man out of the good treasure of his heart brings forth good, and an evil man out of the evil treasure of his heart brings forth evil. For out of the abundance of the heart his mouth speaks

The key observation here is, 'out of the abundance of the heart, the mouth speaks' which is why the instruction is so strong guarding our hearts.

 It's also strong guidance *for people to look at the outward appearance, but the Lord looks at the heart (**1 Samuel 16:7**)*
The subconscious Mind (Heart) is who YOU are;
This is your individuality, your "I AM" so to speak (made in God's image), your "heart".

We all know the first time IAM was used when God instructed Moses on how He should be called. God says I AM ("I AM WHO I AM"), and the Hebrew says, "Ehyeh asher Ehyeh", which translates as "I will be what I will be."

When God then tells Moses, "Say this to the people of Israel: *I AM has sent you*" **(Exodus 3:14)**

It's in the IAM that we see the power and glory of God, and His grace unfold. Jesus used IAM **7 times** in his ministry.

1. The Bread of Life

*John 6:35 And Jesus said to them, **"I am the bread of life**. He who comes to Me shall never hunger, and he who believes in Me shall never thirst."*

The manna that God offered to the Israelites in the wilderness is to foretell that Jesus – the true bread of life will be fed to all those who hunger for His Word.

Manna	Jesus
Supernatural food sent from heaven to satisfy the physical hunger of the people for a **limited time**	Jesus the bread of life sent from heaven, satisfies not only the Physical hunger but also the Spiritual hunger **eternally**
Our fathers ate the manna (which **lasts for less than a day**) that was sent from heaven in the wilderness, and **they died**	The **living bread (eternal)** that came down from heaven; if anyone eats this bread, will **live forever**
Israel **rejected** God's provision of **manna** from heaven	The world rejected **Jesus**, God's provision of the ultimate bread from heaven.

- o Jesus, the Bread of Life, fed the multitude, just by multiplying the 5 loaves and 2 fish (7 in total).

- o In Hebrew, Beth(בֵּית) means House and Lechem(לֶחֶם) means Bread. Jesus was destined to be born in Bethlehem (Beth + Lechem = House of Bread) for He is the **House** that has the **Bread** to feed his children for life.

It's important to see the character of God and His purpose as he orchestrates the journey from the Old Covenant of Law & and prophets to the New Covenant of Love, Grace, and Truth, i.e. Jesus Christ.

2. Light of the World

*John 8:12 Then Jesus spoke to them again, saying, "**I am the light of the world**. He who follows Me shall not walk in darkness, but have the light of life."*

Psalm 119: 105 **Your word** is a lamp for my feet, a light on my path.

The Psalmist in this scripture indicates that God's word is a lamp to our feet and a light to our path. God's Word is none other than Jesus. Darkness is being away from the Truth for the Truth is what sheds light over all darkness and Jesus is the Truth.

3. The Door

*John 10:9 "**I am the door**. If anyone enters by Me, he will be saved, and will go in and out and find pasture."*

In Exodus 12:22-23 there is an instruction to Moses for the Passover on how they can be saved from the Angel of Death (the destroyer) who is after the soul. We can see the same correlation with Jesus.

In the Passover Event, there was a sacrificial lamb without blemish, in whose blood the hyssop was dipped and applied to the lintel and the 2 doorposts. The Israelites were to be inside the house and not step outside the door. In the Passover event that occurred in the New Testament, Jesus became the sacrificial lamb without blemish (sinless), in whose Blood the hyssop when dipped and applied to the lintel and doorposts of our lives, we are saved. The same condition applies that we need to be inside the door. Just like Noah was instructed to stay inside the Ark so that he and his family would be saved, similarly all that stay in this Ark (Jesus) and do not step outside the door (Jesus) will be saved.

He chose hyssop, the meek and humble plant to represent who He truly is, meekest of all.

4. Good Shepherd

John 10:11 **"I am the good shepherd.** *The good shepherd gives His life for the sheep."*

- Jesus the Son of God became the Son of Man
- The King became a servant
- The King chose a donkey to ride instead of a horse
- He who was to be served came to serve
- He who is rich became poor for us
- The Shepherd became the Lamb to be slain
- He who is Life became Death for our sake
- He who is blameless became Sin for us
- He chose to die, so that through His death we may live forever

5. The Resurrection and Life

*John 11:25-26 Jesus said to her, **"I am the resurrection and the life. He** who believes in Me, though he may die, he shall live. And whoever lives and believes in Me shall never die. Do you believe this?"*

Though He died for our sins, He rose that we may be justified and boldly come in to access God's throne of mercy.

With the resurrection, he gives life to our mortal bodies, so that with His second coming, we are raised with Him as our resurrected bodies.

6. The Way, the Truth, and the Life

*John 14:6 Jesus said to him, "**I am the way, the truth, and the life**. No one comes to the Father except through Me."*

Jesus is the door that leads to the Father and in Revelation 3:8 it indicates that God will put before us an open door which no one can shut. This open door is Jesus, through Him, we have access to God. He is the right way; He is the Truth and He provides us eternal life.

7. *The Vine*

*John 15:5 "**I am the vine**, you are the branches. He who abides in Me, and I in him, bears much fruit; for without Me you can do nothing."*

The command given to mankind was to be Fruitful. Roots don't bear fruits, Vine doesn't bear fruits. It's the branches that produce fruit. So, for us as branches to produce fruit, we need to rely on the Vine, for it is the source of supply of all nourishment to the branches so that we can produce good fruit. The branches need to relate to the vine to be able to be fruitful. If not, they are thrown into fire and burned, for our purpose is not met.

A beautiful revelation here is that all these 7 IAMs were only listed in John's gospel.

Was it because He was the disciple that Jesus loved, so He was the only one spoken to about these powerful IAM affirmations?

'The disciple whom Jesus loved' is mentioned 5 times, guess in which Gospel? Gospel of John only. Isn't it amazing? Jesus didn't declare that He had any favorite disciples, however, John professed not his love for Jesus but how much Jesus loved Him.

Indeed, a great learning to be able to see more revealing truths about the gospel. May be a good reason for John to have his way and not in line with the synoptic gospels (Matthew, Mark & Luke). Additionally, John is the one to have recorded the book of Revelation.

Similar account of David, who is claimed to be the man after God's heart. In the book of Acts, the apostle Paul speaks of God's feelings about King David: *"After removing Saul, he made David their king. He testified concerning him: 'I have found David son of Jesse, **a man after my own heart**; he will do everything I want him to do'"* (**Acts 13:22**).

David proved his Faith in God every time and in everything praised God in thanksgiving. Though David committed adultery and murder, the 2 most grave sins, his repentance, and his faithfulness cleared his accounts to be reconciled with God. He is recorded as the one who wrote more than half of the Psalms, more offered as Thanksgiving.

Both David and John seem to have extraordinary and supernatural encounters with great revelation of the mysteries of the Spiritual Realm.

Let's also discover and apply the power of IAM

Let's check on the 2nd part of the Soul, i.e Will

Will is the willingness to make a choice. By the free will that we have, we are always presented with:

2 choices - right or wrong

2 paths - right or wrong

And 'will' is that ability to stand firm and make the choice that is befitting as the Child of God, i.e. the right choice.

Let's look at examples from the Bible that indicate the presence of will and how it was exercised.

Will of Adam & Eve: Adam and Eve were the first male and female that God created, who had a will and all the provisions they had access to, including our destiny – Eternal Life through the Tree of Life – Jesus Christ but chose to eat the forbidden fruit from the Tree of knowledge of Good and Evil and chose Physical and Spiritual Death.

So, here's how they chose to use their most precious free will to pick up the wrong path.

Most times, I have wondered and have also been asked this question:

If God hadn't tempted Adam and had only told him that he was permitted to eat from all trees and not prohibited him from eating that one tree, maybe he wouldn't have been disobedient and sinned.

First clarification: God doesn't tempt. How sure am I about it? I'm sure because it is written as:
James 1:13 Let no one say when he is tempted, "I am tempted by God"; for God cannot be tempted by evil, nor does He tempt anyone.
Secondly, to explain it further, we can take the example of a parent who tells their child to play with all kinds of toys but not to go near the fire or touch it.

But if the child leaves all the toys behind, inquisitively goes near the fire and touches the flame and as a result, burns its hands, should the parent be blamed for it? There is always a consequence for disobedience.

The parent will always advise about the good and warn about the evil. More than the child feeling hurt by the burn, the parent will suffer from that consequence. In the same manner, God, the Father, suffered the most when Adam disobeyed and hurt himself by getting mankind detached from the creator, as God cannot stand in the presence of sin.

This means Adam lost his soul to Satan for the price of mankind

And therefore, it's written:

Psalm 49:8 *For the redemption of his soul is costly*

Since the redemption of the soul is costly, there was only 1 priceless, precious ransom that God chose - His will.

It was the Blood of Jesus that was shed for the redemption of sins, sickness, salvation of souls & for all the evil that was traded for mankind's soul.

1 Peter 1:18-19 For you know that it was not with perishable things such as silver or gold that you were redeemed from the empty way of life handed down to you from your ancestors, but with the precious blood of Christ, a lamb without blemish or defect.

Psalm 142:7 "Bring my soul out of prison, that I may praise thy name"

So, the soul that was lost was redeemed from the prison of Satan, when Jesus won the victory over the gates of hell and triumphed over death.

The 3rd part of the Soul is the emotions/feelings.

Emotions These are sentiments that are felt in our senses and expressed through our body.

From the below verse, we understand that God knows all our feelings and thoughts and hears every word that comes from our mouths. So, nothing is hidden from the one who created us.

*Wisdom 1:6 Wisdom is a spirit that is friendly to people, but she will not forgive anyone who speaks against God, for God **knows our feelings and thoughts**, and hears our every word.*

Examples from the Word of God on emotions:

- o Belongs to earthly nature- sexual immorality, impurity, lust, evil desires, greed, anger, rage, malice, slander, and filthy language from our lips.

- o Belongs to the Spiritual/divine nature - fruits of the Spirit are love, joy, peace, forbearance, kindness, goodness, faithfulness, gentleness, and self-control.

The consequence of emotions is stated in this scripture:

Proverbs 15:18 A hot-tempered person stirs up conflict, but the one who is patient calms a quarrel.

And here's the instruction for our minds to prosper:

Romans 12:2 Do not conform to the pattern of this world, but be transformed by the renewing of your mind. Then you will be able to test and approve what God's will is — his good, pleasing, and perfect will

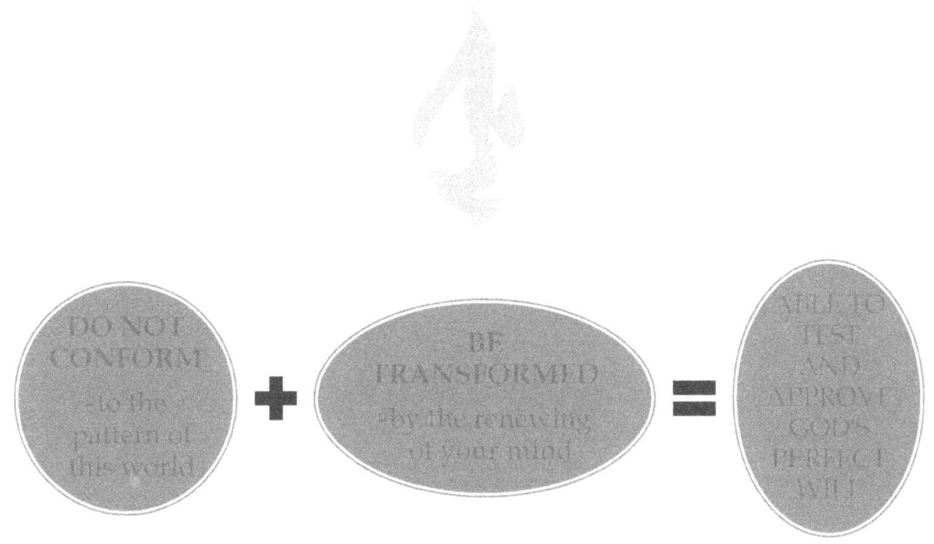

The secret equation again:

Also, another instruction:

Colossians 3:2 *Set your minds on things above, not on earthly things.*

This is very well illustrated with Noah's ark where the ark didn't have any windows just an opening at the top (roof), so the ones

inside the ark wouldn't be worried about their situation, the floods surrounding them, but only one option to set their minds on things above and look above to the One who is the solution. It had a **door** for the people to **enter the rest** that the Lord provides.

Genesis 6:16 *Make a **roof** for it, leaving below the roof an opening one cubit high all around. Put a **door** in the side of the ark and make lower, middle and upper decks.*

God, is the only solution for every situation

Now, all this understanding should help us answer the questions:

- o What would anyone gain from obtaining our soul?
- o Why only the souls of humans and not of other creation?

Chapter 3: Knowing the Destination

The Lord directs my steps

׳ (Yod)

When we have now embarked on this soulful journey, we need to know where we are headed, and what is our destination.

Any journey has 2 paths: right or left
Any journey has 2 choices: right or wrong

Let's learn more about the right choice and the right path to reach the right destination.

As we learn the Word of God, you will see the relevance of the number **Two** and how that is connected to the destination set for us.

*Sirach 33:14 Good is the opposite of **evil, life** is the opposite of **death**, and **sin** is the opposite of **devotion to the Lord**. Think about it: the Most High has **made everything in pairs**, each thing the opposite of something else*

Here's everything about the pairs from the Word of God:

More to the Power of Two

Two Witnesses

Revelation 11:3 And I will grant authority to my <u>two witnesses</u>, and they will prophesy for twelve hundred and sixty days, clothed in sackcloth."

*John 8:17 Even in your law it has been written that the testimony of **two men** is true.*

Two Daughters

Genesis 19:8 Now behold, I have <u>two daughters</u> who have not had relations with man; please let me bring them out to you, and do to them whatever you like; only do nothing to these men, since they have come under the shelter of my roof."

Two Angels

*Genesis 19:1 Now the **two angels** came to Sodom in the evening as Lot was sitting in the gate of Sodom. When Lot saw them, he rose to meet them and bowed down with his face to the ground.*

Two Animals

*Genesis 6:20 **Two of every kind** of bird and animal and crawling creature will come to you to be kept alive.*

Two Cities

*Jude 1:7 just as **Sodom and Gomorrah** and the cities around them, since they in the same way as these indulged in gross immorality and went after strange flesh, are exhibited as an example of undergoing the punishment of eternal fire.*

Two Disciples

*Mark 6:7 And He *summoned the twelve and began to send them out **in pairs**, and gave them authority over the unclean spirits;*

Two Groups

*Genesis 32:7 Then Jacob was greatly afraid and distressed, and he divided the people who were with him, and the flocks and the herds and the camels, into **two groups**;*

Two Great Lights

*Genesis 1:16 God made the **two great lights**, the greater light to govern the day, and the lesser light to govern the night; He made the stars also.*

Two Doorposts

*Exodus 12:7 Moreover, they shall take some of the blood and put it on **the two doorposts** and on the lintel of the houses in which they eat it.*

Two Tablets of Stone

*Exodus 32:15 Then Moses turned and went down from the mountain with the **two tablets** of the testimony in his hand, tablets which were written on both sides; they were written on one side and the other.*

Two Commandments

*Matthew 22:40 On these **two commandments** depend all the Law and the Prophets.*

Two Covenants

Galatians **4:24** *which things are symbolic. For these are the two* <u>covenants</u>: *the one from Mount Sinai which gives birth to bondage, which is Hagar*

Two Sons

Genesis **10:25** <u>*Two sons*</u> *were born to Eber; the name of the one was Peleg, for in his days the earth was divided; and his brother's name was Joktan.*

Galatians **4:22** *For it is written that Abraham had* <u>*two sons*</u>, *one by the bondwoman and one by the free woman.*

Genesis **41:50** *Now before the year of famine came,* <u>*two sons*</u> *were born to Joseph, whom Asenath, the daughter of Potiphera priest of On, bore to him.*

Matthew **21:28** *"But what do you think? A man had* <u>*two sons*</u>, *and he came to the first and said, 'Son, go work today in the vineyard.'*

Luke **15:11-31** *Then Jesus said, "A man had* <u>*two sons*</u>.

Two robbers

Matthew **27:28** *Then* <u>*two robbers*</u> *were crucified with Him, one on the right and another on the left.*

The only place where **<u>two are blessed to become one</u>** is in the below verse:

Ephesians **5:31** *For this reason a man shall leave his father and mother and shall be joined to his wife, and the* **<u>*two shall become one flesh*</u>**.

We are always presented with **<u>2 choices</u>**:

Eating:
Genesis **2:9** *In the middle of the garden were the* **tree of life** *and the* **tree of the knowledge of good and evil**.

Eternal Life (Tree of Life)	Eternal death (Tree of the knowledge of good and evil)
Free to eat from **any tree**	Must **not eat** from the **tree of the knowledge of good and evil**

Serving:

Matthew 6:24 No one can serve two masters; for either he will hate the one and love the other, or he will be devoted to one and despise the other

One master (God)	Second Master (Wealth)
Serve God	Serve wealth
Love one	Hate the other
Devote to one	Despise the other

You cannot serve God and wealth.

Following:

1 Kings 18:21 Elijah came near to all the people and said, "How long will you hesitate between two opinions? If the Lord is God, follow Him; but if Baal, follow him.

First Opinion (God)	Second Opinion (Baal)
Follow God	Follow Baal

There are **<u>2 paths</u>** that we need to choose from:

Way of Righteousness (Good)	Way of Unrighteous/Wicked (Evil)
Like a tree planted by streams of water, which yields its fruit in season	**Like chaff** that the wind blows away
Do not walk in step with the wicked	
Does not stand in the way that sinners take	**Will not stand** in the judgment of the righteous
Do not sit in the company of mockers	
Delights are in the law of the Lord and meditates on his law day and night	

There are <u>**2 outcomes/consequences to the choices:**</u>

Consequence to the right choice & right path	Consequence of the wrong choice & wrong path
The leaf does not wither	Leaf withers
Whatever you do prospers	You shall die
Blessed & Fruitful	Burning the chaff with never-ending fire
Eyes of the Lord are on the righteous	The face of the Lord is against those who do evil
Heaven	Hades

1(The choice that we make) + 1 (The path that we take) = 2 (Decides the outcome)

What and how do we choose then?

Jesus simplifies this for us through the Word which specifies 2 gates, The Narrow and Wide Gates

Matthew 7:13-14

"Enter through the narrow gate. For wide is the gate and broad is the road that leads to destruction, and many enter through it. But small is the gate and narrow the road that leads to life, and only a few find it.

With this, we know what to choose:

- o   The narrow gate/The path of the righteous

John 14:6 For Jesus is the Way, The Truth, and the Life

- *The Way* is what Jesus teaches us to follow the path of the righteous through the narrow gate, not the one leading to **destruction**
- *The Truth* is who He truly is – The Son of God, Our redeemer, and savior, protector from the snares of **lies**
- *Life* is what we are led into through Jesus, the tree of life, the destiny that is pre-destined for us, from the trap of **death**.
- What were we pre-destined for?
- What is then our destination?

Ephesians 1:5 He predestined us to adoption as sons through Jesus Christ to Himself, according to the kind intention of His will

This concludes that we were **pre-destined by God** to be **adopted as sons**, i.e. to receive the sonship, the rightful inheritance as children of God, **through Jesus Christ** and this was **His will** for us.

When Jesus came as the **Good Shepherd**, the savior of our souls:

- He redeemed our lives from the power of Sheol and set us for eternal life (*Psalms 49:15*)
- For He will not abandon my soul to Hades, or let His Holy One see corruption (*Acts 2:27*)

However, **Death** will be the shepherd of the sheep that are appointed for Sheol (*Psalms 49:14*)

- Adam was destined for a blessed, fully provisioned, eternal life
- Abraham was destined to be the Father of all nations
- Isaac was destined to obtain the Father's inheritance and to reap a hundredfold in times of famine
- Israel was destined for the promised land
- Moses was destined to lead Israel into the Promised Land
- Joseph was destined to flourish during times of famine and be catapulted to be at the right hand of Pharoah

- Jonah was destined to bring salvation to the people of Nineveh
- Jesus was destined to save the world through His death & and resurrection from all that is not from God

We were destined as the seed of the first Adam to be partaking in the abundance prepared for us, however, through the wrong choice made by Adam, our souls were abandoned to Hades.

Through the second and last Adam, Jesus Christ, with the redemption of our souls, has now restored us to the same destiny as designed by the creator.

Destination involves a journey. The journey involves choices. The decision to make the right choice should always depend on God, for He created the destination and orchestrates the journey. We understand the reliance on God through the below verse.

Judges 18:5-6 *Then they said, "**Ask God** whether or not our journey will be successful." "Go in peace," the priest replied. "For **the LORD is watching over your journey.***

*1 Corinthians 2:7-9 But we impart a secret and hidden wisdom of God, which **God decreed before the ages for our glory**. None of the rulers of this age understood this, for if they had, they would not have crucified the Lord of glory. But, as it is written, "What no eye has seen, nor ear heard, nor the heart of man imagined, what **God has prepared for those who love him**"*

Now that we understand our destiny and destination, let's also understand how this came about.

We were earlier taught that:

- Satan sinned
- He caused mankind to sin through deception
- Sin separated mankind from God
- There was a need for redemption
- Jesus was destined to become sin so that we could be made the righteousness of God in Christ

Here's the verse to indicate how sin/iniquity becomes a barrier between God and us.

Isaiah 59:2 But your iniquities have made a separation between you and your God, and your sins have hidden his face from you so that he does not hear.

God cannot see sin and therefore the **first sacrifice was made by God** to cover sin.

Genesis 3:21 The LORD God made garments of skin for Adam and his wife and clothed them.

So, throughout the journey in the Old Testament, sacrifices and offerings were made for the riddance of sins.

The **five** types of offerings in the Old Testament.

- The Burnt Offering
- The Grain Offering
- The Peace Offering
- The Purification Offering
- The Reparation Offering

5 is the number of Grace (ה) 5th alphabet in Hebrew (Hei) to foretell of the Grace that was to come through Jesus Christ, who would become the ultimate sacrifice and the covering for all offerings.

*John 1:17 For the **law** was **given through Moses; grace and truth came** through **Jesus Christ**.*

*Hebrews 10:5 Consequently, when Christ[a] came into the world, he said, "**Sacrifices and offerings** you have not desired, but a body have you*

prepared for me; in burnt offerings and sin offerings you have taken no pleasure. Then I said, 'Behold, I have come to do your will, O God, as it is written of me in the scroll of the book.'

Hebrews 10: 11-12 *And every priest **stands daily** at his service, offering **repeatedly** the **same sacrifices**, which **can never take away sins**. But when **Christ**[b] had **offered** for **all time a single sacrifice** for sins, he **sat down** at the right hand of God*

In the letter to the Hebrews, we understand that God does not desire sacrifices and offerings, for these could not fulfill any law nor take away sins.

Here's a startling Truth with the distinction of offerings of Priest and Christ:

Every Priest	Christ as a High Priest
Offers repeatedly the same sacrifices	Offered for all time a single sacrifice
Can never take away sins	Took away all sins
Stands daily	Sat down
Unfinished – Had to be offered repeatedly	Finished - Once and for all

Further in the scriptures, we see that the Holy Spirit bears witness to us:

Hebrews 10: 17-18 "*I will remember their sins and their lawless deeds no more.*" *Where there is forgiveness of these, there is no longer any offering for sin.*

With the ultimate sacrifice by Christ, once and for all, our sins are wiped out, therefore there is no longer an offering for sin. With the new covenant, God doesn't remember our sins and lawless deeds anymore.

What a beautiful promise!

Chapter 4: Understanding our navigation system

The presence of God goes with us and gives us rest

כ (Kaff)

With every destination comes a journey and with every journey comes the unknown.

If the destination we are headed to is not a familiar one, we would need a guide, a compass, or a navigation system.

In this special teaching, we will learn the continued inspiration of the guide, who leads us and guides us along the right paths.

First, let's try to understand the features of a good navigation system:

- Route planning
- Turn by Turn directions
- Offline Maps
- Lane Guidance
- Noise cancellation
- Voice assistance

Where can we find a good navigation system for our journey to reach the destination we are called to? Let's find out in the Truth guide.

- **Route planning**

Any trip/journey requires good planning. The system will guide you to the necessary path as well as automatically reroute you if you deviate from the initial course. Plus, you can usually see the history of your trips and choose to repeat them or backtrack.

*Isaiah 58:11 The LORD will **guide you** always*

*John 16:13 But when he, the Spirit of truth, comes, he will **guide you** into all the truth*

Psalms 32:8 I will instruct you and teach you in the way you should go

Through these scriptures, we understand that the Holy Spirit is our navigation system, always ready to guide us and instruct us in the way we should go. The choice to follow or reroute is completely ours.

- **Turn by Turn directions**

Turn-by-turn directions include visual data on the screen along with voice instructions, so your attention can remain on the road. The system voices the direction of the turn, street names, and the distance to the next turn. It can also warn you about traffic congestion and toll roads ahead.

Just like the Holy Spirit voiced to Jesus that it was Satan speaking through Peter, similarly, with every turn, every step, we are vulnerable to a wrong turn. He guides us to keep our focus on the right path and warns us of the temptations ahead.

He enables us to keep our eyes on the Truth (The Word of God) along with voice instructions.

Psalms 37:23-24 The LORD makes firm the steps of the one who delights in him; though he may stumble, he will not fall, for the LORD upholds him with his hand.

- **Offline Maps**

Unfortunately, you can't always rely on a cell connection, especially when you travel to remote areas. So, an offline map is among the most essential features of a good navigation system.

God is our strong tower, the source of all supply.

Like an internet tower that transmits connection to all users, God transmits His power through the Holy Spirit in us.

The tower is stable and doesn't move. The potential for us to lose connectivity is when we distance ourselves from the tower. When

we distance ourselves, we become easy targets for our enemy, Satan.

While on this journey, we may lose connectivity, if we falter along the paths and that's exactly when the offline map comes in handy.

The Holy Spirit will remind us of everything that we have been taught so we can declare/meditate on these offline methods to regain our direction and set off on the right path again.

Proverbs 4:11 *I have directed you in the way of wisdom; I have led you in upright paths.*

- **Lane Guidance**

This is a driving assistance that alerts you when you're driving too close to the car in front or when you're drifting out of the lane, specifies which lane you should be in, and switches to camera view when you're approaching your destination.

Satan is driving too close to you, for he watches us to attack us/devour us. To find that one vulnerable moment when we drift out of the lane and succumb to failure.

This is exactly when the Holy Spirit alerts us and gets us to the lane we should be in, switches our attention to the view where we are aware of the love of our Father and that we are close to our destination.

Psalm 121: 3, 7-8 He will not let your foot slip

he who watches over you will not slumber;

The Lord will keep you from all harm — he will watch over your life; the Lord will watch over your coming and going both now and forevermore.

Deuteronomy 31:8 "And the Lord, He is the One who goes before you. He will be with you, He will not leave you nor forsake you; do not fear nor be dismayed."

- **Noise cancellation**

An advanced navigation system must make sure it can hear you no matter what: whether there's an open window, children screaming in the back seat, or your spouse singing to your right (or left).

The only difference here is it's not God or the Holy Spirit that has to make sure they hear us, but we have to be unclogged and have our ears open to hear from Him.

Ears would mean both physical and spiritual.

There are many voices as we travel and it's important to be focused on that voice and be able to discern amidst all the noises around us.

Job 37:2 Hear attentively the noise of his voice, and the sound [that] goeth out of his mouth.

Samuel also had to discern the voice of the Lord amongst Eli's voice. When the voice called to Samuel later that night, he answered, *"Speak; for thy servant heareth"*

(*1 Samuel 3:10*).

If Eve had canceled that noise from the serpent, she would have heard God clearly and stayed put on his command of not eating from the forbidden tree and being able to live the destined eternal, abundant life.

- **Voice assistance**

This is for the traveler to be able to use voice commands for the system to direct them to the right destination. It also enables voice-based routing to keep you focused visually and allow your ears to guide the vision.

Isaiah 30:21 Whether you turn to the right or the left, your ears will hear a voice behind you, saying, "This is the way; walk in it."

This verse exactly describes the voice assistance feature as installed on our systems (body sensors).

Revelation 3:20 Here I am! I stand at the door and knock. If anyone hears my voice and opens the door, I will come in and eat with that person, and they with me.

Psalm 48:14 For such is God, Our God forever and ever; He will guide us until death.

When we talk about repentance, it means turning back to God. It's resetting not resenting, it's rerouting not resisting the right path that was directed to us by the Holy Spirit. The one we chose to take but midway, wavered and took the wrong path. Repentance is the choice we make to take a

you turn back on the right path. To make a choice and listen to the voice amidst the noise.

Here's a quick traveler's tip: A Tip for the Trip

*Exodus 13:21 The Lord was **going before them** in a pillar of cloud **by day** to **lead them on the way**, and in a pillar of fire **by night** to give them light, that they **might travel by day and by night**.*

This tip teaches us to stay faithful to our ever Faithful God. The one who:

- Goes before us
- Leads us
- Gives us light/direction
- Watches over us all the days of our life
- Watches our going and coming now and forevermore

This is to acknowledge the most efficient inbuilt navigation system we have in the Holy Spirit. We can never fail, never falter, never waver, if we follow His voice, be willing to follow his guided paths, and arrive in pomp and glory to our Destination.

Throughout the journey from the old covenant to the new covenant, we have strong evidence of our God's faithfulness that our God has neither forsaken nor left us.

Chapter 5: Meditating in the Heart

Ponder on His Word Day and night

ל (Lamed)

In the earlier chapters, we have read about the subconscious mind and its power to control our journey. We learned about acts of faith and prayer and how they activate the access to the Spiritual Realm.

In this chapter, we will learn more about the subconscious mind (heart) and how we can be successful in reaching the destination using tactics of meditation. How the power of meditating in the heart can obtain for us all desires of the heart.

Ephesians **1:18** *Having the* **eyes of your hearts** *enlightened, that you may know what is the hope to which he has called you, what are the riches of his glorious inheritance in the saints,*

1 Corinthians **2:9** *But, as it is written, "What* **no eye has seen***, nor* **ear heard***, nor the* **heart of man imagined,** *what God has prepared for those who love him"*

Matthew **13:13** *This is why I speak to them in parables, because seeing they* **do not see***, and hearing they* **do not hear***, nor* **do they understand.**

2 Kings **6:20** *Elisha said, "O Lord,* **open the eyes** *of these men, that they may see." So the Lord opened their eyes and they saw, and behold, they were amid Samaria.*

Matthew **13:15** *For this* **people's heart has grown dull***, and with their* **ears they can barely hear***, and their* **eyes they have closed***, lest they should see with their eyes and hear with their ears and understand with their heart and turn, and I would heal them*

Opening eyes to spiritual reality is what these scriptures indicate.

- Physical Eyes are opened to see the spiritual reality
- Spiritual Eyes are closed when the ability to see is affected by the heart condition

So, what changes a person, is their ability to see, which is the knowledge of things around you. When we perceive the situation around us and see things that are shown to us or through the situation, our response determines the level of sight we have and that's the same information we feed to our heart.

This means it's important to learn the art of activating our spiritual senses.

The main step to activate Spiritual eyes is to meditate. In most scriptures, it's meditating in the heart.

Psalm 19:14 *"Let the words of my **mouth** and the **meditation of my heart** be acceptable in your sight, O LORD, my rock and my redeemer."*

*Joshua 1:8 This Book of the Law shall not depart from your **mouth**, but you shall **meditate in it day and night**, that you may observe to do according to all that is written in it. For then you will make your way prosperous, and then you will have good success.*

And since we are learning about the heart, it's more meaningful to learn about meditation as well as understanding the relevance of **mouth, heart, and meditate** as you can observe in the above scriptures.

What is Meditation?

There are various kinds out there teaching meditation in a worldly way. That's the way I was aware of too until I was awakened to the Biblical meditation.

Meditate in Hebrew means hagah, i.e., utter or mutter a low sound. So, when the **mouth** speaks, our ears hear and our **heart** visualizes (**meditates**) and then out of the abundance of the heart the mouth speaks.

Since our spirit man has been trained, it's time to **train the soul.**

Why train the soul?

If our souls are receiving and processing information based on the senses that are connected to the world, out of its information and the abundance in the heart, the same information will flow from the mouth. And we are familiar with words being spirits, so we need to deposit the right quality of content in the heart, so the mouth can pick up only that which means the words spoken can only bring forth goodness and the right fruit.

As the psalmist says:

Psalm 119:11 *I have hidden your word in my heart that I might not sin against you*

So, depositing the Word of God in our heart is the only way to keep away from the wiles of the devil and when the heart is full of the Word and the mouth is full of praises for God (Psalms 71:8), there is no room for the worldly word.

Let's see an example of 'Meditating in the Word of God' from the Word of God.

Genesis 24:62 He (Isaac) went out to the field to **meditate**, and as he looked up he saw camels approaching.

Key points:

- **Why meditating in the field?**

Isaac returned from Beer-lahai-roi and went to the field to meditate, the same place where Haggah was previously blessed to bear Ishmael (*Genesis 16:14*). It means, 'the well of him that lives and sees me'

- Place where prayers were answered

What was he meditating on?

Meditating on the outcome he knew that they had gone to seek a bride for him.

Result:

Success in finding a godly partner, Rebekah

How to meditate?

- Pick any verse from the Bible
- Start meditating (pondering and muttering) on it repeatedly
- Breakdown the verse
- Write down what He tells you as you are being taught by the Lord
- Ask questions and draw pictures

Let's understand the application based on an example:

- **Pick any verse: Here's my favorite one**
  - *John 3:16 For God so loved the world that He gave his only begotten Son, so that whosever believes in Him will not perish but have everlasting life*

- **Start meditating by reading the verse in its entirety**
    - o In case you are not in a place where you can write, memorize the verse
- **Break it down into fragments**
    - o *1 For God 2so 3loved the world that 4He gave 5His only begotten Son, so that 6whosever believes in Him 7will not perish 8 but have everlasting life.*

We have broken down the verse into 8 fragments:

- **Write down what the Lord is teaching us**
- **Ask questions**
    - o I'm doing both these actions side by side

Questions:

- Who loved?
  God
- How much did God love?
  So much
- Whom did he love?
  Loved the world
- What is the proof of his love?
  He gave his only begotten Son. No pressure as they say. He decided, His choice, therefore, He gave.

- What is the result of his love?
  Whosoever believes in Him will not perish but have everlasting life for that is our destiny.

Here's how the secret equation works:

$$1 \quad + \quad 1 \quad = \quad 2$$

For God so loved the world that He gave his only begotten Son	Whosever believes in Him	Will not perish but have everlasting life

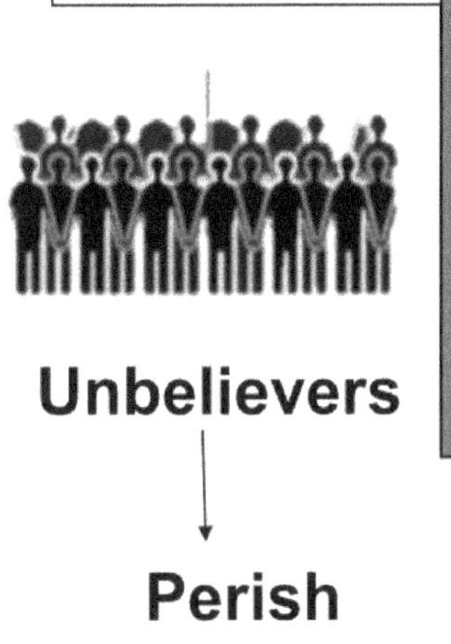

God's choice:
Gave His only begotten Son

Our choice:
Believe in Him

Unbelievers

Believers

Perish

Eternal Life

Related verse: *Genesis 3:16,* looks like quite a beautiful plan unfolding right?

Genesis 3:16	John 3:16
*Then God said to the woman, "I will cause you to have **much trouble when you are pregnant,** and when you **give birth to children, you will have great pain***	*For **God so loved the world** that **He gave his only begotten Son,** so **that whosever believes in Him will not perish but have everlasting life***

Here is the Revelation #1:

In Genesis, God is speaking of himself that He will have a lot of trouble when He needs to separate His Only-begotten Son (for the wrath and judgment that was to come) and when He gives birth or brings forth Jesus and delivers His son into the hands of the world. He will be in great pain, however, just like a mother who is in pain while giving birth but when the baby is in her arms, she rejoices. In the same way, God cut off his right arm (Jesus) and was in pain when He separated from Him due to the sins of the world. However, that separation was soon converted into reunion with his resurrection, and He is seated at the right hand of the Father or is the Father's right arm.

This is the choice God made for mankind.

Do you want to see another revelation that was shown to me?

Revelation # 2:

- # of commands in the Bible are: 613
- Reversal of the law/commands: 316
- God is love, so He can only give love
- In every law we need to find love

So, 316 is the true definition of true love.

Revelation # 3:

How about another equation in the revelation?

3 is the number of the Triune God

1 is the number of the union/Unity

6 is the number of mankind

3	: 1	6
The Triune God separated Himself from His Son	Became One to be with mankind as **God** with us, Word in flesh **(Jesus)** and the Spirit	For the atonement of mankind's sins

Isn't that precious? However, God might have provided proof of his love with His action.

- What is the proof of our Faith?

As the verse says, our only part is to Believe and thereby Receive.

In my case, there are several testimonies that you'll read about in my Psalms section.

Romans 10:9 *I confess with my mouth that Jesus Christ is Lord and believe in my heart that God raised Him from the dead and we are saved.*

This is the formula for the salvation of souls.

Since we have now better understood the heart, mouth, and meditation, with the correlation between them, it is also good to learn about the other term for the heart which is the subconscious mind, which is not termed anywhere in the Bible like that but the context is that of the subconscious mind.

The Hebrew word found in Scripture is "cheder," which means the inward part, the hidden chambers, or the secret place.

Proverbs 20:27, *"The spirit of man is the candle of the Lord, searching all the inward parts (cheder) of the belly."*

Of the many scriptures talking about the Subconscious mind, this is apt to what we are learning in this section.

- Again, why would the spirit search our inward parts, if not to reveal hidden sin in us, to us?

Psalm 51:6 Behold, You desire truth in the innermost being, And in the hidden part [of my heart] You will make me know wisdom.

Now, if we relate both the above verses,

The Spirit searches our inward parts to be cleansed of secret faults/sins and then be filled with God's Wisdom.

So, we must empty ourselves to be filled with His wisdom and His promises

James 1:21 Therefore, putting away all filthiness and overflowing of wickedness, receive with humility the implanted word, which can save your souls.

How do we know if our mind is renewed?

Like we did the 'born again" test for our spirit, here's the test to check if the mind is renewed or not.

- Do your thoughts control you?
- Is your mind filled with unforgiveness, bitterness, and things of the past?
- Are you unable to replace your thoughts of the 'World' with the 'Word'?

If the answer is, 'No' to the above, congratulations, 'You have renewed your mind'

How do we know God is on our side? He is not the one who created death or sent sickness. How can, we be sure?

1 Timothy 2:3-4 *God our Savior, who wants all people to be saved and to come to a knowledge of the truth.*

*2 **Peter** 3:9 The Lord is not slow in keeping his promise, as some understand slowness. Instead, he is patient with you, not wanting anyone to perish, but everyone to come to repentance.*

Wisdom 1:13 because God did not make death,

and he does not delight in the death of the living.

For he created all things so that they might exist;

the generative forces of the world are wholesome,

and there is no destructive poison in them,

and the dominion of Hades is not on Earth.

These scriptures bring out the Truth about who God truly is and His will for us.

- He is our **savior**
    - So wants all his people to be **saved** and come into the knowledge of the truth
    - He is **patient** and therefore despite our grave sins doesn't want **anyone to perish** but **everyone to come to repentance**
    - He did **not make death** for He **created all 'good' things**

HOLY SPIRIT AS WATER

PHYSICAL

REALM

(BODY)

3

HOLY SPIRIT AS WATER

Mayim (מַיִם)

in Hebrew means **water**. In the beginning, of *Genesis 1*, we see that the Spirit of God was hovering over the **waters**. In the end, *Revelation 21*, It is written that to the thirsty He will give water without cost from the spring of the **water of life**.

The waters that God created cover 70% of the earth's surface and so does our **body** taken from the dust (earth) is comprised of 70% water. This is not just a scientific reality but a divine truth where if our bodies don't get the desired quantity and quality of water, they can get dehydrated and eventually die. The Holy Spirit provides our **body** with the most essential nourishment, the living **water**.

Chapter 1: What is the purpose of the Body?

For the glory of the creator

מ (Mem)

Our bodies are holy because God made them, and everything God makes has a purpose.

Ephesians 2:10 For we are His workmanship, created in Christ Jesus for good works, which God prepared beforehand that we should walk in them

1 Corinthians 6:20 For you were bought at a price; therefore glorify God in your body and in your spirit, which are God's.

We were bought with a price, in other words, our bodies have been ransomed for a price.

- How do we know the ransom has been paid?
- How do we know that we are redeemed?
- What was the ransom?
- Ransom has been paid

*1 Timothy 2:5-6 For there is one God, and one mediator also between God and men, the man Christ Jesus, **who gave Himself as a ransom for all**, the testimony given at the proper time.*

- We are redeemed:

*Titus 2:14 who **gave Himself for us** to **redeem us** from every lawless deed, and to purify for Himself a people for His possession, zealous for good deeds.*

- Ransom was the Precious Blood of Jesus shed for us

*Acts 20:28 Be on guard for yourselves and for all the flock, among which the Holy Spirit has made you overseers, to shepherd the church of God which He **purchased with His blood**.*

- Why was Jesus chosen as the Redeemer, when there were so many anointed prophets and men of God?

In the Old Testament, redemption involves deliverance from bondage based on the payment of a price by a redeemer. The Hebrew root words used most often for the concept of redemption are pada, gaal, and kapar. The verb pada is a legal term concerning the substitution required for the person or animal delivered.

This explains why we needed a substitute and why animal sacrifices prevailed.

*Hebrews 2:14 Since the children have flesh and blood, **he** too shared in their humanity so that by his death he might break the power of him who holds the power of death – that is, the devil and free those whom all their lives were held in slavery by their fear of death. For surely it is not angels he helps, but Abraham's descendants. For this reason, he had to be made like them, fully human in every way, so that he might become a merciful and faithful high priest in service to God, and that he might make atonement for the sins of the people.*

- 'He' mentioned in the above scripture is Jesus
- He came in flesh and blood for we were in flesh and blood
- Through his death, He broke the power of the devil who holds the power of death to bring freedom to the ones destined for death
- He did all this as an atoning sacrifice for the sins of the whole world

*Hebrews 3:3 Jesus has been found worthy of **greater honor than Moses**, just as the **builder of a house** has **greater honor** than the **house itself***

*Hebrews 1: 3 Every **high priest** is selected from among the people and is appointed to represent the people in matters related to God, to **offer gifts and sacrifices for sins.** He can deal gently with those who are ignorant and are going astray since he is subject to weakness. This is why **he has to offer sacrifices for his sins, as well as for the sins of the people***

Hebrews 20-28

Let's understand from the scriptures why Jesus was the right choice for mankind.

Prophets and chosen people of God	Jesus Christ
Moses as the house	As the builder of the house
Every High Priest has to offer sacrifices for his sins, as well as for the sins of the people	Jesus who knew no sin became sin for us
Others became priests without any oath	Because of God's oath, Jesus has become the guarantor of a better covenant
There have been many of those priests since death prevented them from continuing in office	Jesus lives forever, he has a permanent priesthood
For the law appoints as high priests men in all their weakness	The oath, which came after the law, appointed the Son, who has been made perfect forever

This is why it summarizes the need for Jesus as our **only Savior** and **Redeemer.**

- He can **save completely** those who come to God through him because **he always lives** to intercede for them
- He **truly meets our need** — one who is holy, blameless, pure, set apart from sinners, exalted above the heavens
- Unlike the other high priests, he **does not need to offer sacrifices day after day**, first for his sins, and then for the sins of the people
- He sacrificed for our sins **once and for all** when **he offered himself**

Additionally, here's why **Jesus** could be the **only one** to redeem us.

A redeemer needs to qualify on 3 grounds:

- Must be rich
- Must be willing
- Must be a relative

Let's check for the qualification of Jesus to meet these criteria:

- **Rich**:

2 Corinthians 8:9 For you know the grace of our Lord Jesus Christ, that though He was rich, yet for your sakes He became poor, that you through His poverty might become rich.

Jesus Christ is the Son of the Most High God, the creator of Heaven and Earth, King of the universe, not only **rich** in mercy but in **heavenly riches**.

- **Willing**:

Matthew 8:2-3 A man with leprosy came and knelt before him and said, "Lord, if you are willing, you can make me clean."

*Jesus reached out his hand and touched the man. "I am **willing**," he said. "Be clean! "Immediately he was cleansed of his leprosy.*
Jesus was **ever willing** to heal the sick, raise the dead, cleanse lepers, and cast out demons

- **Relative:**

Galatians 4:7 Therefore you are no longer a slave, but a son; and if a son, then an heir through God.

Son of God became the Son of Man so that we the Son of Man can become the Son of God. So, we have now become heirs through God and are no longer slaves.

Additionally, we now understand that spirits need a body to operate legally on Earth.

Here's the bonus learning:

'Christ – The Spirit' needed a body to operate on Earth to be legal.

*Hebrews 10:5 Therefore, when Christ came into the world, he said: "Sacrifice and offering you did not desire, but a **body you prepared for me***

As per the above scripture, **Christ** (Spirit) came into the world, God prepared the body for Christ. The **Body** that was named Jesus.

When it comes to understanding the purpose, the most inspirational verse for me is *Matthew 25:14-30* where I realize talents (could be a skill, money, time, etc) are given by God **according to our ability**.

If I'm entrusted with **<u>time</u> as a talent**, how well have I managed it in the past will determine my ability to receive more of it or do more with it.

If I'm entrusted with **<u>skill</u> as a talent**, how I have used this skill in the past will determine the opportunities I now get to use this skill, according to my ability to perform.

If I'm entrusted with **<u>money</u> as a talent**, how well I have accounted for it in the past determines my ability to receive it.

According to the below scriptures, we understand that once God provides us with these talents according to our ability, we need to provide an account of all that we did with them.

*Romans 14:12, "So then **each of us** shall give an **account of himself** to God."*
*Luke 9:10-17 When the apostles returned, they gave an **account to Him of all that they had done***

Chapter 2: Understanding Our Body

Our Body is the temple of the Holy Spirit

נ (Nun)

1 Corinthians 12:12-26 *A person has **only one body**, and the **body has many parts**. It is the same with Christ. The One Spirit baptized us **all to make one body**. It made no difference whether we were Jews or Greeks, whether we were slaves or free men. We were all given to drink of one Spirit. I say again, the body is not all one part, but has many parts.*

Perhaps the foot says, `I am not the hand, so I do not belong to the body.' But it is still a part of the body.  Perhaps the ear says, `I am not the eye, so I do not belong to the body.' But it is still a part of the body.

If all of the body were an eye, how could we hear? If all the body were an ear, how could we smell? The way it is now, God has put each part of the body in the place he wanted it. If they were all one part, how could it be a body? The way it is now, there are many parts, but it is one body. The eye cannot say to the hand, `I do not need you.' And the head cannot say to the feet, `I do not need you.' No, that is not so. Some parts of the body are not as strong as others. Yet we could not live without them. And we look after some parts of our body more than others because they need it. The parts of our body that are not so fine in one way are made more fine in other ways. But the parts which are fine already do not need to be made fine. God made the body and has given more care to the parts that need it.

He did this so that the body would not be divided into groups, but all the parts would help each other. If one part has trouble, then all the other parts are troubled too. If one part is praised, then all the other parts are glad with it. Now, all of you together are the body of Christ, and each one of you is a part of it. God has given each person their right place in the church. First, there are the apostles. Second, some prophets speak words from God. Third, some teach. Then some do big work. Then some have the gifts to heal people, those who help in the work of the church people, those who lead and guide others, and those who speak God's words in different kinds of tongues or languages.

This is such an enriching Truth.

The body has many parts that have **different functions**	**All the children of God** are **together in the body of Christ**, with **different gifts** given by the Holy Spirit
yet are **united and not divided into groups**	Irrespective of faith, caste, and other **differences, are to be united**
but **created to help each other and work in unity**	but **created to help each other and work in unity**
to achieve the purpose of the body	Are **meant to help in the work of the body**, i.e Jesus Christ

We must understand the different parts of the body and their purpose/functions as per the Word of God:

Body Part	Function
Eye	*Matthew 6:22* *"The **eye** is the lamp of the body. So, if your eye is healthy, your whole body will be full of light*
Ear/Heart	*Proverbs 22:17-18* *Incline your **ear**, and hear the words of the wise, and apply your **heart** to my knowledge, for it will be pleasant if you keep them **within you** if all of them are ready on your lips.*
Tongue/Lips	*1 Peter 3:10 For, "Whoever would love life and see good days must keep their **tongue** from evil and their **lips** from deceitful speech*
Mouth	*Ephesians 4:29 Do not let any unwholesome talk come out of your **mouths**, but only what helps build others up according to their needs, that it may benefit those who listen.*
Hands	*Acts 6:6 And these they brought before the apostles; and after praying, they laid their **hands** on them*
Feet	*Proverbs 4:26 Watch the path of your **feet** And all your ways will be established.*
Heart	*Proverbs 4:23 Above all else, guard your **heart**, for everything you do flows from it.*

In summary:

- The **eye** is the lamp of the body and should be healthy and give light to the whole body.
- The **ear** should always hear the instruction of the wise
- This instruction is then stored in the **heart** and the heart is guarded
- Since everything flows from the heart, the **mouth** speaks from the abundance of the heart which helps build others according to their needs
- The **tongue** chooses to speak well and the lips don't lie
- All that the **hands** do prosper, and they lay hands on the sick to share the prosperity
- The **feet** go places sharing the good news of the Lord

These body parts though different, come together to share in the glory and for the purpose for which they were created. The **eye** *sees His goodness*, the **ear** *inclines to His teaching*, the **heart** *rejoices with gladness in the Lord*, the **mouth** *sings His praises*, the **tongue** *confesses that Jesus Christ is Lord*, the **knee** *bows in worship*, the **hands** are *raised high to exalt the Lord*, to *surrender to His mighty presence*, the **feet** are *dancing like David to the wonders of the Lord*.

There are consequences for not doing the act/part that you are called to do. If we read the below scriptures, we understand what is the consequence of not acting according to the Word. Not to be viewed as punishment but as training, correction, and teaching to refine our character.

*Proverbs 6:16 There are **six things** that the **Lord hates**, **seven** that are an **abomination to him**: ¹ haughty eye, ² a lying tongue, and ³ hands that shed innocent blood, ⁴ a heart that devises wicked plans, ⁵ feet that make haste to run to evil, ⁶a false witness who breathes out lies, and ⁷ one who sows discord among brothers.*

*Matthew 18:8-9 If your **hand or your foot** causes you to stumble, cut it off and throw it away. It is better for you to enter life maimed or crippled than to have two hands or two feet and be thrown into eternal fire. And if your **eye** causes you to stumble, gouge it out and throw it away. It is better for you to enter life with one eye than to have two eyes and be thrown into the fire of hell.*

If these parts do not perform the function for which they were created, 'unfruitful'. Just as the fig tree though could produce fruit didn't serve the master with its fruits, it was cursed and withered by its roots, so shall be the destiny of such parts that do not function in the way they should.

The body is designed for a purpose on Earth. When the purpose is fulfilled, the body goes back to dust, from where it came. It has no identity. When someone dies, they stop referring to the body with the name of the person. For example: They would say,
" Bring the body to the cemetery" and not, "Get Mr. Francis to the cemetery".

During his tenure on earth, Jesus went about healing the sick 'bodies', driving the demons out of the 'bodies' because these 'bodies' were designed for a definite purpose, not for housing sickness and demons. All our days are numbered, and the purpose is decided. It is for us to be clear on understanding the purpose, live accordingly, and die when the purpose is accomplished. Just like Jesus said, "It finished" when His purpose on earth was completed, we need to yearn to do and say, "It finished" when we complete the purpose for which we were called.

Romans 8:28 And we know that in all things God works for the good of those who love him, who have been called according to his purpose.

So, we understand that we have all been called according to a purpose and these have been prepared by God in advance for us to accomplish (*Ephesians 2:10*).

Chapter 3: Flesh vs Body

Walk by the Spirit and not the flesh

ס (Samekh)

This is what I recently understood:

Flesh and Body are 2 different things.

Let's read from the scriptures what is the difference between these 2, i.e Flesh and Body

Flesh:

*Genesis 2:22-24 Then the Lord God made a woman from the rib he had taken out of the man, and he brought her to the man. The man said, This is now the bone of my bones and **flesh of my flesh;** she shall be called 'woman,' for she was taken out of man." That is why a man leaves his father and mother and is united to his wife, and they become **one flesh**.*

***Galatians* 5:16-17** *So I say, walk by the Spirit, and you will not gratify the desires of the **flesh**.*

For the desires of the flesh are against the Spirit, and the desires of the Spirit are against the flesh, for these are opposed to each other, to keep you from doing the things you want to do.

***John* 6:56** *Whoever eats my **flesh** and drinks my blood remains in me, and I in them.*

Body:

***James* 2:26** *For as the body apart from the spirit is dead, so also faith apart from works is dead.*

1 Corinthians 15:44 It is sown a natural body; it is raised a spiritual body. If there is a natural body, there is also a spiritual body.

Through the scriptures, we understand that Flesh and Body are 2 different aspects.

Flesh is contrary to the spirit. For a believer, flesh disagrees with the Spirit as the ways of flesh is carnal and the ways of the Spirit are Spiritual. For an unbeliever, their flesh agrees with the spirit as they lack knowledge of the indwelling Spirit of God within them.

Like Paul indicates in the below scripture as believers, we are born again, our old self is crucified with Jesus so that the **body** of sin (**flesh**) is brought to nothing, so that we are no longer slaves of sin.

Romans 6:6 We know that our old self was crucified with him so that the body of sin might be brought to nothing so that we would no longer be enslaved to sin.

Talking about flesh, I learned that we are given a thorn in our flesh. We have Paul confirm this with the below scripture:

*2 Corinthians 12:7-9 Therefore, to keep me from becoming conceited, I was **given a thorn in my flesh, a messenger of Satan**, to torment me. Three times I pleaded with the Lord to take it away from me. But he said to me, "My grace is sufficient for you, for my power is made perfect in weakness."*

Let's understand this a bit more.

Since we have learned about the body parts and their different functions, we can relate to them as a family/team/community.

Just like different body parts have different functions but are still connected to the same body.

- A family is also designed to stick together with different family members of different mindsets
- A team is also comprised of different team players with different abilities
- A community is a fine collaboration of different cultures and different diversities in union with each other

- Even the fingers of our hand are designed so differently that though different in size, function uniformly.

Have you wondered if our fingers were all the same size or our family of the same temperament or a like-minded team or a same culture community would it have made life easy?

We would think so but no. There would be no variety of thoughts, no different views, the same thinking, no challenges and so would make man very comfortable in his space. Not getting refined to be made gold/diamond or anything precious for these stones become precious because of their ability to thrive in extreme conditions. The ability to be molded and the willingness to change is what refine a character.

MY THORN IN THE FLESH: Through this journey in the Lord with the guidance of the Holy Spirit, I learned that there is a thorn in the flesh given to me too.

This makes so much more sense now than when I initially used to react to anything coming from this person contradicting the Word of God. I kept correcting their ways only to know this was just not working. This also impacted rather impeded my journey with the Lord, for the bitterness and anger kept growing inside of me.

Though I chose to forgive I didn't forget and eventually realized that I hadn't forgiven for if I had forgiven, I should have forgotten and my burden felt lighter, and my bitterness disappeared. It didn't. It just grew. As I was writing this book, it was when I read through this verse, or rather it was revealed through this verse that it was a test. A test to not just let me survive but thrive, to not just win but be victorious, to rise above all things. Not just having all the right people and situations around me, but someone/something that distracts me/irritates me that I can either chose to stay on track or easily get sidetracked.

I also realize the underlying meaning of the thorn in the flesh. It would be how irritating it would be to have a thorn in your flesh. You would want it out at any cost so it stops bothering you. With the attempt to remove it, you would be hurting yourself more, but the thorn wouldn't be removed. There have been times when I said, "Why Lord, just if this person is not around, I would be the perfect child".

The best route would be to stop allowing it to distract you, stop allowing it to bother you and grow more powerful in the Lord, that someday you realize it's no longer there.

In the ways of the stone test, I could either be refined as a precious stone or be discarded as the waste for I remained a stone and now charred for I couldn't withstand the test.

I have chosen to withstand the test and emerge as the precious stone that I'm designed to be.

This could also relate to any situation at the workplace/neighborhood/community. If you are aware that there is a thorn in the flesh, you also know the purpose that Paul shared with us (*2 Corinthians 12:7-10*)

HIS GRACE IS SUFFICIENT FOR ME

Chapter 4: Understanding the Law

Law is fulfilled by love

ע (Ayin)

To get started, we need to know where we see the legal system operating. Which Realm would this apply to?

Back to the source of all information, i.e. The Word of God or in legal terms, let's refer to the Constitution.

Let's look for the legal terms used across:

Dates to the Torah or the books of **law** or instruction, a Hebrew word meaning "to teach" and spanning across the New Testament.

The Ten Commandments or the laws	The appointed Judges	Testimony
2-3 Witnesses	Lawsuits	Adversary
Decree	Judgment	Absolute
Accusation	Acquit	Adopt
Advocate	Justice	Appeal
Plea	Petition	Approve
Arbitrary	Assault	Assets
Lawyers	Authority	Blasphemy
Bond	Bondsman	Case
Charge	Condemn	Condition
Consideration	Contempt	Counselor
Court	Covenant	Customary
Declaration	Witness	Guilty

Of the many roles that **God** plays, He is known for being the 'Right and Just Judge'.

As a judge who only seeks justice for His people, He has defined a legal/judicial system for His people and as a judge given them the law and will judge them according to the law.

2 Corinthians 5:10 – For we must all appear before the judgment seat of Christ, so that each of us may receive what is due us for the things done while in the body, whether good or bad.

This confirms that there is a judgment that will take place and we will receive what is due to us for the things done in the body, whether good or bad.

Let's look at other scriptures to find out why He introduced a legal system and what is He trying to teach us through this.

*Isaiah 33:22 – For the **Lord is our judge**, the Lord is **our lawgiver**, the Lord is our king; it is he who will save us.*

God is our judge, and He is also the lawgiver and His main purpose is to save us.

God exhibits Wrath against Sin. Because of God's holiness, he cannot tolerate sin. The Bible says that "the wages of sin is death" (**Romans 6:23**). God's wrath is poured out on those who reject him.

Let's also try to understand these aspects:

- Why was the law given?
- How was the law fulfilled?
- What was the divine judgment?
- What are the consequences of not abiding by the law?

With the below scriptures, we understand that we could never fulfill the law and are never able to meet God's standard and need Grace and a Saviour who could redeem us. The one who can mediate and give us justice.

Galatians 3:19 Why, then, was the law given at all? It was added because of transgressions until the Seed to whom the promise referred had come. The law was given through angels and entrusted to a mediator. A mediator, however, implies more than one party; but God is one.

Galatians 3:23 Before the coming of this faith,[j] we were held in custody under the law, locked up until the faith that was to come would be revealed. So the law was our guardian until Christ came that we might be justified by faith. Now that this faith has come, we are no longer under a guardian.

So in Christ Jesus, you are all children of God through faith, for all of you who were baptized into Christ have clothed yourselves with Christ. There is neither Jew nor Gentile, neither slave nor free, nor is there male and female, for you are all one in Christ Jesus. If you belong to Christ, then you are Abraham's seed, and heirs according to the promise.

*Galatians 4:4 But when the set time had fully come, **God sent his Son, born of a woman, born under the law, to redeem** those under the law, that we might receive **adoption to sonship**.[b] Because you are his sons, God sent the Spirit of his Son into our hearts, the Spirit who calls out, "Abba,[c] Father." So you are no longer a slave, but God's child; and since you are his child, God has made you also an heir.*

This tells us that every law had to be fulfilled and therefore the prophesy for the redeemer to be born of flesh and blood was done according to the law for we were under law and not Grace.

Grace gave us the ability to call God as, Abba Father through the Spirit in our hearts.

We are adopted to sonship and now an heir in Christ.

Of the 613 commands in the Bible, the Holy Spirit indicates great learning through some specific ones.

Law given	Law fulfilled
Unclean Food *Leviticus 20:25* *You shall therefore separate the clean beast from the unclean, and the unclean bird from the clean. You shall not make yourselves detestable by beast or by bird or by anything with which the ground crawls, which I have set apart for you to hold unclean.*	**Food declared clean** *Mark 7:18-19 And he said to them, "Then are you also without understanding? Do you not see that whatever goes into a person from outside cannot defile him, since it enters not his heart but his stomach, and is expelled?" (Thus he declared all foods clean.)*
Leprosy (Unclean & Untouchable) *Leviticus 13:45 A diseased person(leper) must wear torn clothes and let his hair hang loose,b and he must cover his mouth and cry out, 'Unclean, unclean!' As long as he has the infection, he remains **unclean**. He must live alone in a place outside the camp.*	**Healed <u>by Touch</u>** *Matthew 8:2-3 And behold, a leper came to him and knelt before him, saying, "Lord, if you will, you can make me clean." And Jesus **stretched out his hand and touched him**, saying, "I will; be clean." And **immediately his leprosy was cleansed***
Bleeding (Unclean & Untouchable) *Leviticus 15:19-33* *"Whenever a woman has her menstrual period, she will be ceremonially unclean for seven days. Anyone who touches her during that time will be unclean until evening.*	**Healed <u>by Touch</u>** *Matthew 9:20-22* *Just then a woman who had been subject to bleeding for twelve years came up behind him and touched the edge of his cloak. he said to herself, "If I only touch his cloak, I will be healed."* *Jesus turned and saw her. "Take heart, daughter," he said, "your faith has healed you." And the woman was healed at that moment.*
Dead (Unclean & Untouchable) *Numbers 19:11* *"Whoever **touches the dead body** of any person shall be **unclean** for **seven** days.*	**Healed <u>by Touch</u>** *Mark 5:41 He **took her by the hand** and said to her, "Talitha koum!" (which means "Little girl, I say to you, get up!"). 42 Immediately the girl stood up and began to walk around (she was twelve years old).*
Circumcision: Of the flesh *Genesis 17:10–14* *This is my covenant which you shall keep, between me and you, and also with your offspring after you: Every male among you shall be circumcised. And you shall **circumcise the flesh of your foreskin**, and it shall be a sign of the covenant between me and you.*	**Circumcision: Of the heart** *Colossians 2:11–12* *In whom also you were circumcised with a **circumcision not made by hands**, by the removal of the body of the flesh, by the **circumcision of Christ**, having been buried with him in baptism, in which also you were raised together with him through faith in the working of God, who raised him from the dead.*

Through each of these, we understand,

- All that was declared unclean, and untouchable was made clean through Christ and His touch (Be it food or leprosy or discharge or touching the dead body).

We also understand that Jesus came to fulfill the law and not abolish the law.

Now, that we know that God is a rightful Judge and a keeper of the law and Jesus was the only Redeemer who could redeem us, let us understand the lawful process.

Isaiah 13:9 – See, the day of the Lord is coming – a cruel day, with wrath and fierce anger – to make the land desolate and destroy the sinners within it.

So, there is a day when the wrath and fierce anger of God (divine judgment) was to come and Jesus came as the substitute for we were dead in sins, unable to contend with the adversary.

Like the foretelling of substitution through Abraham's test of faith when **Isaac** (His one and only son) has a **substitute** with a **ram** to be offered as a burnt offering. Similarly, **our substitute** was the lamb, God's One and Only Son- **Jesus Christ**.

The substitute had to be a male without defect.

God made Him (Jesus Christ) who knew no sin to be sin on our behalf so that we might become the righteousness of God in Him

(2 Corinthians 5:21)

- As a substitute, what did Jesus do?

Who: The adversary (1 Peter 5:8)

What: Charged us with legal indebtedness, this debt stood against us and condemned us. (Colossians 2:14)

Plea: Canceled the charge of this indebtedness, took it away, and nailed it to the cross (Colossians 2:14)

Verdict: We are guilt-free and disarmed from the powers and authorities

Other bonus verdict:

Romans 8:2 *"For the law of the Spirit of life has set you free in Christ Jesus from the law of sin and death."*

Romans 6:14*"For sin will have no dominion over you, since you are not under law but under grace."*

When Job was slapped with an accusation by the adversary, he had no mediator.

*Job 9:33-35 **If only** there were a **mediator** between us, someone who could bring us together. The **mediator** could make God stop beating me, and I would no longer live in terror of his punishment. **Then I could speak to him without fear**, but I cannot do that in my strength.*

However, unlike Job, we have a mediator:

1 Timothy 2:5-6 *There is one God **and one mediator** so that human beings can reach God. That way is through Christ Jesus, who is himself human. He gave himself as a payment to free all people. He is proof that came at the right time.*

So, we now have proof that Jesus came as a human, as a mediator to fulfill the requirements of the law (body on earth) cancel the accusations, and make the payment in full through His precious Blood so that we are no longer under slavery of sin but redeemed to Grace.

Just like it's easy for us to declare independence and live a life of freedom, we need to freely apply this to our lives as Children of God.

The Law has been fulfilled through Christ

The law also was fulfilled through the Birth, His life, Death, and Resurrection.

Law/Prophesy in the Old Testament	Fulfilled in the New Testament
Birth of Jesus: *Isaiah 7:14* — Isaiah prophesies that a pure young woman will give **birth** to God's son	*Matthew 1:18-23* — Isaiah's prophecy is fulfilled with the **birth** of Jesus, Son of God through Mary, the virgin young woman
Circumcision: *Leviticus 12: 3* *On the eighth day, the boy is to be **circumcised***	*Luke 2:21 Eight days later, Jesus was **circumcised***
Male firstborn dedicated to the Lord: *Exodus 13:2 **Consecrate** to me all the firstborn.*	*Luke 2:23 his parents took him to Jerusalem to **present** him to the Lord*
Purification Offering *Leviticus 15:29* **On the eighth day,** she shall take **two turtledoves, or two young pigeons,** and bring them to the priest, to the door of the Tent of Meeting.	*Luke 2:24 On the eighth day: and to offer a sacrifice according to that which is said in the law of the Lord, "A **pair of turtledoves, or two young pigeons.***"
Death of Jesus: *Isaiah 53:5 But he was pierced for our transgressions, he was crushed for our iniquities; the punishment that brought us peace was on him, and by his wounds we are healed."*	*1 Peter 2:24 "He bore our sins" in his body on the cross, so that we might die to sins and live for righteousness; "by his wounds you have been healed."*
Resurrection of Jesus: *Jonah 1:17"The Lord had prepared a great fish to swallow Jonah. And Jonah was in the belly of the fish three days and three nights."*	*Matthew 12:39-40"An evil and adulterous generation seeks after a sign, and no sign will be given except the sign of the prophet Jonah. For as Jonah was three days and three nights in the belly of the great fish, so will the Son of Man be three days and three nights in the heart of the earth.*

Likewise, there are many scriptures in the Bible that validate the just Judge, God making sure that He lives according to the law and His Word is fulfilled according to the requirements of the law that is set.

He didn't shy away from having His Son, be the one to fulfill all the requirements of the law on our behalf, so that through the mediator, we can get justice. Not by our works but by His.

Matthew 5:18 For truly I tell you, until heaven and earth disappear, not the smallest letter, not the least stroke of a pen, will by any means disappear from the Law until everything is accomplished"

Now, that we have been redeemed and enjoy freedom, we are called to be joyful, not just once but always.

- How can you always be joyful?
- What is the hidden secret here?

Philippians 4:4 Always be full of joy in the Lord. I say it again – rejoice!

1 Thessalonians 5:16-18 Be joyful always, pray at all times, be thankful in all circumstances.

Let's create a court scene:

In the courtroom, we have:

Role	Action
Judge	The ultimate authority to provide judgment
Accused/ Defendant	The person against whom the charge is and needs to defend themself
Accuser/ Adversary/ Plaintiff	A person who brings a charge against another in a court of law
Advocate	Represents the client in a court of law and argues their case on their behalf
Counsel/ Lawyer	A person who gives advice and deals with various issues, particularly in legal matters
Interpreter	Conveys in one language literally what has been said by the other, without additions, omissions
Witnesses	An individual called to testify or provide evidence in a trial

Now, that we know the different roles in a courtroom, let us understand how this is positioned in the Spiritual Realm and how we ensure the verdict is in our favor.

Role	Supported verse
God Judge	***Psalm 75:7*** *But **God** is the **Judge**; He puts down one and exalts another*
Humankind Accused/ Defendant	***Zechariah 3:1*** *Then he showed me Joshua the high priest standing before the angel of the Lord, and Satan standing at his right hand to **accuse** him.*
Satan Accuser/ Adversary/ Plaintiff	***1 Peter 5:8*** *Be sober, be vigilant; because your **adversary** the **devil** walks about like a roaring lion, seeking whom he may devour.* ***Luke 18:3*** *A widow was in that city, and she often came to him, saying, 'Defend me from my **adversary**!'*
Jesus Christ Advocate	***1 John 2:1*** *My little children, I am writing these things to you so that you may not sin. And if anyone sins, we have an **Advocate** with the Father, **Jesus Christ** the righteous*
The Holy Spirit Counsel/ Lawyer	***John 14:26*** *But the **Counselor**, the **Holy Spirit**, whom the Father will send in my name, he will teach you all things and will remind you of all that I said to you*
The Holy Spirit Interpreter	***Romans 11:34*** *"For who has known the mind of the Lord? Or who has been his **counselor**?"* ***1 Corinthians 2:11*** *You are the only one who knows what is in your mind, and **God's***

	Spirit is the only one who knows what is in *God's mind*.
The Holy Spirit Witnesses	*John 1:7 He came as a **witness**, to testify about the Light, so that all might believe through him.* *Acts 5:32 And we are **witnesses** of these things; and so is the Holy Spirit, whom God has given to those who obey Him."*

Ultimately, the courtroom (heavenly courts) is a complete setup to ensure the children of God get justice for which He has appointed:

- Jesus as the Advocate, who represents us and fights our case
- Holy Spirit as the Counsel, Interpreter who counsels and interprets in Spirit. He is also the witness for He is the Spirit of Truth and Truth is what prevails in a court of law.

Isn't that a powerful fool-proof setup which means there is no way we could ever lose a case as the favor of God is upon us with Jesus and the Holy Spirit contending for our victory.

When there is a hearing, The Judge is interested in evidence, witnesses, and if it fulfills the requirements of law.

In this case, there was a charge of legal indebtedness by the Adversary, i.e Handwriting of requirements which is the obligation mentioned by God for His people to abide by in the Book.
The evidence had to prove that all the requirements were met.

Evidence: Blood of the Lamb was shed for the forgiveness of the sins of the whole world and death was defeated on the Cross.

Deuteronomy 19:15 "A single witness shall not rise against a man on account of any iniquity or any sin which he has committed; on the evidence of two or three witnesses a matter shall be confirmed.

As humankind, we inherited sin from Adam and were indebted through our lawless deeds to meet the lawful requirements defined by Mosaic law or defined by God's law. This is the legal indebtedness that kept us away from our true inheritance. This

charge had to be removed. Previously, there was an attempt made to remove through the blood of animals but it was to be annually done and the charges could not be removed.

When the Blood of the Lamb was shed, every sin, every dominion, every bondage was broken.

- The payment for the charges was done
- The ransom was paid
- The redemption was made

All with one mighty evidence – The Precious Blood of Jesus shed once and for all, for the forgiveness of the sins of the whole world.

There is no condemnation for those in Jesus Christ.

Now, let's check how the secret formula works: Remember, this is how prayer (petition) works and must be in the courtroom and not on the battlefield.

James 4:7 Submit yourselves, then, to God. Resist the devil, and he will flee from you.

<table>
<tr><td align="center">1</td><td align="center">+</td><td align="center">1</td><td align="center">=</td><td align="center">2</td></tr>
<tr><td align="center">Submit to</td><td></td><td align="center">Resist the</td><td></td><td align="center">he will flee</td></tr>
<tr><td align="center">God</td><td></td><td align="center">devil</td><td></td><td align="center">from you</td></tr>
</table>

1) Submit to God:

- Approach the Judge (**God**)
- Submit your case (**petition**)
- Use the sections from the constitution (**Word of God**)
- Since we don't understand the constitution (**Word of God**) so well, we take with us our Lawyer (**Jesus**) to provide the evidence (**His Blood**)
- Our Advocate (**The Holy Spirit**) brings to our remembrance all things that our lawyer (**Jesus**) had said to us
- As the **accused, cancel** the words that the devil holds as testimony binding you (all false testimony)
- The **Holy Spirit** will **testify** and stand as our **witness**

2) **Resist the devil:**

- o Rebuke the devil (Just as Jesus used the words from the constitution, use the Word to fight against his word)
- o Use the tactics we learned earlier on identifying the adversary and his evil motives and resist him

3) **He (devil) will flee from you:**

- o The evidence of two or three witnesses and the matter has been confirmed
- o Declare the victory
- o For we are now justified

***Romans* 8:33** *Who shall bring any charge against God's elect? It is God who justifies.*

A reminder that in any formula, if either of the process steps are not followed, it will not end in the desired result.

Reasons for the formula not to work:

- o **Step 1 not followed**: Did not submit to God
- o **Step 1 followed but not Step 2**: Submitted to God but did not resist the devil
- o **Mixed up the formula or altered the result**: Fled from the devil

Don't try to alter the result. Follow the process steps diligently.

Another formula as we celebrate our victory:

*Revelation 12:11 And they **overcame him** by the **blood of the Lamb** and by **the word of their testimony***

1	+	1	=	2

Blood of the	Word	We have
Lamb	of our	overcome
	testimony	Satan

 God's part   +   Our Part   = Desired result

What a revelation from Revelation right?

- o Here, Step 1 is a constant – Jesus's work: Finished/Accomplished
- o Step 2 is our part which needs to also be fixed for the required results

The Evidence of God's Love for us was giving His Only Son to save the world through His precious Blood

What is our evidence? What is the proof that we believe He is the savior, that we trust His Finished works?

It must be our Faith. No greater thing pleases God than faith itself (*Hebrews 11:6*).

Mark 11:24 *Therefore I tell you, whatever you ask for in prayer,* **believe** *that you have received it, and* **it will be yours**.

Gratitude is the 'seen' evidence before the 'unseen' Faith comes to be 'seen'

Chapter 5: Union of the Spirit, Soul, and Body

The God of peace Himself sanctifies you wholly

פ (Pei)

From all our teaching so far by the Holy Spirit, we now stand confirmed that:

- We are a Tri-Part being – Spirit, Soul, and Body created in the image and likeness of the Triune God - God the Father, God the Son, and God the Holy Spirit
- Spirit governs the Soul, Soul instructs the Body, Body obeys
- The body of a Born- again Believer fights between the flesh and the Spirit to communicate back to the Soul
- Soul deposits into the Spirit the treasures the Body has passed on

There is a uniqueness, uniformity & and union between these 3 elements (Spirit, Body, and Soul) that are working in co-dependency for the purpose that man was destined, operating in 3 different realms (Spiritual, Intellectual & Physical) for the Glory of the 3 in 1 - Triune God (The Father, The Son, and The Holy Spirit)

Let's reflect on how the beginning in one element and the Realm impacts the other and how the seed sown in one Realm manifests the harvest across different realms.

Matthew 9:22 Jesus turned and saw her. 'Take heart, daughter,' he said, 'your faith has healed you.' And the woman was healed at that moment.

Given the scriptural evidence, it's proven that it's the secret formula at work and a strong connection of the 3 realms at work.

Jesus   +   People/s = Brough forth

The Healer   Faith   manifestation

SPIRITUAL + INTELLECTUAL = PHYSICAL

HIS WORD + HER FAITH   = SHE WAS HEALED

In this scripture, we understand that the healing was always inside of her for the power of healing is always inside the person and so is the Word.

However, for it to manifest or to bring it forth from within had to be activated with FAITH. The moment Faith (Seed) was sown into the Heart (Fertile Soil) with the Word (The fertilizer), it brought forth the Healing (Harvest). You'll see this working in many such examples shared in the Word of God.

In Luke 18:41-42, the blind beggar expressed his desire to see, his words expressed his the desire of what he wanted (To See) rather than what the problem was (could not see).

Though his eyes could not see, his ears had heard about Jesus and his healing power and his faith had increased by hearing and hearing the Word of God (*Romans 10:17*).

This faith that was heard by the ears was deposited into his heart and when he heard that Jesus was passing by, his heart prompted him to express his desire and bring forth the vision through his Faith and by the Word.

His	+	Blind Man's	=	Vision
Word		Faith		restored
(Spirit)		*(Soul)*		*(Body)*

| Receive | + | I want to | = | Your Faith |
| your sight | | See | | has healed you |

Another scriptural example denotes the power working in us and the ability and capacity for the power to manifest.

*Luke 6:18-19 Those troubled by impure spirits were cured, and the people all tried to **touch him** because **power was coming from him** and **healing them all**.*

| Touched | + | Power was coming | = | Healed |
| Him | | from Him | | them all |

| Spiritual | + | Intellectual | | = Physical |
| *(Spirit)* | | *(Soul)* | | *(Body)* |

This is how simple God has made it for the power within us to be manifested with the union of the **3 Realms (Spiritual, Intellectual & Physical)** to unfold into the **3 parts (Spirit, Soul, and Body)** by the power of the **Triune God (Father** who allows the Word that is **Jesus** to be manifested through the **Holy Spirit)**

This brings us to the end of our journey but closer to our destination.

Where we began with, a lack of knowledge, wisdom, and understanding, we now have an abundance of knowledge, on how to use the understanding and apply it.

Proverbs 2:6 For the LORD gives wisdom; from his mouth come knowledge and understanding.

As we continue to use our eye and ear gates to take in the Truth of the Word, store it within our hearts, and allow our mouths to bring it forth, we become Doers and not just Hearers of the Word of God.

To the God-presence, the Spirit that is within us who makes us Fruitful, let us continue in the awareness of the 'Power of IAM' in us.

SECTION FOR PSALMS

When David wrote his Psalms with the other psalmists including Moses, I learned that it was their testimony of the greatness of God and His power in their lives, their thanksgiving, worship, and praise. Their act of remembrance of all the great things done for them.

We all have different situations and are uniquely gifted to handle these situations. All the goodness from the journey of wilderness to the destination of the promised land is a Psalm. Their Psalm cannot be my Psalm unless I have the same situation and the same result.

Here's a series of my Psalms, My Unique testimonies to the glory of God for I cannot and shouldn't forget his benefits.

For my Holy Spirit brought into remembrance all that God had done for my family and me. He has revealed the Truth and the Truth has set us free.

He reminds me that I'm fearfully and wonderfully made and there is no malfunction or malformation in my body. My Spirit has been renewed and My soul prospers.

Psalm of Praise, For by His Grace we are saved

צ (Tsade)

O Father, I sincerely ask of Thee;
One little favour, one little plea.
To make my life devoid of this **cross***
And as an answer, You sent me
Your messenger: That the Truth of life I may see.
He took me to a place where crosses were laid;
In different sizes, for everyone it was made
He asked me to pick up the smallest cross which fitted my need
and paralled my cause

I drifted through the room with a view to fulfil my mission of
possessing the smallest cross of all;
My venture now was getting futile
As no cross could I see;
That could relieve me of burdens and set me free
My head bent low as I almost quit;
My eyes caught the tiniest cross that shone and lit
And I didn't waste time;
In grabbing it in my hold
The shine which lit up my face now seemed to drain;

As I saw the card on it bearing my name
And now as reality dawned on me;
I don't know how to be grateful to thee

And now no more shall I ask for lighter burdens
But will always yearn for stronger backs
For your yoke is easy, and your burden is light
And you have borne it all and set me free
You carried my cross to Calvary
With that you declared victory
Victory over my sickness, victory over my failures,
Victory over my sin, victory over death

You are and always will be 'My Saviour'
The one who called it **'Finished'**

* **suffering**

Psalm of Thanksgiving

ק (Qof)

I need you all the time

I need you for everything

Let me forget all the bad deeds done unto me

Let me forget all the bad thoughts I had

Let me let go of the bitterness in my heart

But let me never forget your good deeds

Let them be engraved on my heart for everlasting & and everlasting, Amen.

Psalm of Praise to the King who chose to die for me

ר (Resh)

I need you all the time

I need you for everything

You told me to give You all **my cares**

I gave them to You and made them disappear into thin air

For You called it Finished

You took these away from me - **Lack, Sickness, Sin** and with your **<u>divine exchange</u>**, you gave me **Abundance, Health, and Righteousness**

I had **Migraine** and doctors gave me medicine to relieve my pain

- You chose to have the <u>**crown of thorns on your head**</u>, O King, that pierced you, not in vain

For by Your wounds, I'm now healed

I was a **sick child**, topped for being the sickest child throughout my childhood and adulthood and various doctors said it was an allergy

- You said you came to **bear my sickness and my iniquities and to set me free**

For by Your wounds, I'm now healed

I had **tonsillitis**, which doctors operated on and cautioned no cold food, and to be away from A/C

- You said **your throat** was dry like a broken vessel and told me to take it easy

For You called it Finished

I used to have a **blocked nose**, with bottles of nasal spray compulsorily by my bedside

- You reminded me of the **Breath of Life** that you breathed into my nostrils and called me your bride

For You called it Good

I had **mouth ulcers** and doctors prescribed vitamins and I glutted down bottles of them

- You sent **Your Word** and healed my disease, my mouth is free from ulcers and has never been the same

For You called it Finished

I had **knee pain**, doctors said knee surgery was the only option

- You reminded me of your bruises and that your Blood was my magic potion

On my knees in Praise of My God

For He called it Finished

I was told I had a heaty body and certain foods were restricted for me

- You said all things made by you are **Good** and blessed them with glee

I glorify the Lord for all things were made by Him and declared Good

For He says it Finished

I immensely suffered from **menstrual pain**, the pangs were too much to bear

- You showed me your body which had no flesh to spare

You gave up your body for me and called it **Finished**

My eyesight got dim and my vision was impaired

- You showed me the blind people whose sight was repaired, and my vision was restored

For You called it Finished

My hunger pangs would strike exactly at the hour and without food, my body would go dizzy like it lost its power

- You showed me how you handled the temptation of food having fasted for 40 days and 40 nights

I control my body now just like you do, For I want to be like You.

For as Jesus is so Am In this world

Praise for planting me in the right garden

שׁ (Shin)

I need you all the time
I need you for everything

What did you plan as you planted me as a tiny seed?

How could I grow into what you planted me to be?

"Be fruitful", You said

"This is very good," You said

You said it was very good and sowed a good seed

You said it shall be fruitful and bear good fruit

And now that's what I have turned to be

A good seed-bearing good fruit in its season

What was sowed in tears is now reaped with joy

Praise You for the garden in which You had me planted

Among good trees and unknown weeds

You blessed me and always have your Spirit in me

Blessed be Your name, now and forever

Thanksgiving for the Grace

ת (Tav)

**I need you all the time
I need you for everything**

Lord, with your mighty hands you planted a tiny me

Among huge trees and plants, tinier I seemed

But then I remembered Adam and imagined what he would have
thought

"Birds of the air, fish of the sea, and every living creature you have
brought

But there is no helper to be found as my partner by my side"

From the man's side came out the woman, the helper she could be

From **Jesus's** side, come out WE, the church for all eternity

And the Church is now the **Body of Christ** with our helper being

the **Holy Spirit** by our side

In the **beginning**,

א

I give **glory to Him** and Him alone

and in the **end**,

ת

To Him belongs all glory and honor,

now and forever

Ah-mayn   Shalom alekhem

אָמֵן   שָׁלוֹם עֲלֵיכֶם

Amen   Peace be upon you